Mother Knew Best
An East End Childho

Dorothy Scannell, who was born Dolly Chegwidden, won an all-London essay writing competition at Woolmore Street Elementary School at the age of twelve. She had written nothing since then until she rashly decided at the age of sixty-three that anyone could write a book. *Mother Knew Best* is the splendid result.

Mrs Scannell now lives in Epping with her husband and has two children and two grandchildren, to whom this book is dedicated.

Dorothy Scannell

Mother Knew Best

An East End Childhood

Pan Books in association with
Macmillan London

First published 1974 by Macmillan London Ltd
This edition published 1975 by Pan Books Ltd, Cavaye Place, London sw10 9pg,
in association with Macmillan London Ltd
© Dorothy Scannell 1974
isbn 0 330 24586 7

Made and printed in Great Britain by
Cox & Wyman Ltd, London, Reading and Fakenham

Contents

To Anne and Matthew Early

1 Just like their mother

'Strong stomachs and weak noses are what your East End teacher needs, never mind brains,' said my father in 1918. I glared at him, thinking he was 'common' to say my friends and I were smelly. Everybody was always going on about being clean. 'It costs nothing to be clean,' our teachers said, and to me it went without saying that if something 'they' were always on about cost nothing, then everybody would have it.

'Cleanliness is next to godliness,' my mother always said when she bathed us on Friday evenings in the little bath before the fire in the kitchen, yet the very next morning she would say, 'You won't want much of a wash today, you had a bath yesterday.' And on a winter's day she would say, 'Don't wet your face, just wipe it, going out into the cold, because of the chaps.'

My father would always shout one of his remarks when I was thinking nice thoughts. I felt he didn't like the lovely Poplar people. 'What about the Lascars then?' he'd say. Apparently these thin brown-skinned men who roamed the High Street carried little tin cans of water around with them. My father said proudly, 'They wash down below every time they go to the lavatory, it's their religion.' I thought it was a funny religion, for 'down below' was bottoms, and they didn't get dirty, for they were covered with bloomers or trousers; so how could the dirt get there? Suppose one of the Lascars made a mistake one day and washed his down below before washing his face. Mother always said on bath nights, 'I must wash your face first.' I would hate to walk about with a can of water all my life, it would get rusty, and the water would get muddy. Suppose our family were Lascars, that would mean twelve cans of water. There was nowhere in our little kitchen to put twelve cans of water, and what a terrible thing if they all got mixed up. Ugh, fancy washing your face in someone else's can if they'd washed their bottom in it first. Anyway my brothers all kicked tin cans about in the street, so we couldn't keep twelve cans.

My father was always going on about smells. 'Watch your drains,' he would shout. I always made a detour away from any drain, or held my breath, so that I would not get the fever and be taken away in a scarlet blanket. I thought this blanket was red so that people would know you were dangerous, like a leper, and the fever was named after the blanket, scarlet fever, but we all called it THE FEVER in horrified whispers. There was even a hospital, a terrible place, called the Fever Hospital, where you were taken and not allowed home until all your skin had come off.

Once I had shingles all round my neck, except for a little space, and my brother Cecil, two years older than me, said that when my shingles met I would die. Everybody dies when shingles meet. Mother put some white rag round my neck and I went out to play. When we heard that Johnny Duggan was being taken away with the fever we all went to watch. The red blanket covering Johnny had missed his big toe which looked enormous: his nail wanted cutting and the edge of it was all black. My brother David, two years older than Cecil, gave me a push while I was watching the fever boy and I fell on the red blanket. Johnny's toenail, the black part, caught a shingle on my neck and broke it and made it wet and sore. 'You won't have to wait for the shingles to meet now,' said David cheerfully. 'You'll have the fever instead.' I ran home crying to Mother because I didn't want the fever, and I still might die with meeting shingles, and Mother put some 'brassic' powder on my neck. I didn't get the fever. No one did in our house.

My father always seemed to spoil my pleasure with one of his common remarks. When my younger sister Marjorie was old enough to be my friend one of our favourite adventure places was Harrow Lane Station, down a steep slope off the High Street. We would chase down the cobble-stoned slope up the iron stairs to the wooden footbridge and feel all lovely and swaying as we peeped through the chinks in the wooden slats of the bridge at the trains passing beneath. When a train drew into the station then the exciting part would begin, for when the train began to start again it would get up loads of lovely steam which would shroud our part of the bridge. We would get into the steam and let it envelop us all over our legs and over our faces and then we would dash to the other side to catch the last of the steam before the train got up speed. We didn't know that Father had seen us in our Turkish bath one day and when we arrived home he shouted, 'That steam from the engines down Harrow Lane is no good for young girls. Your mother should keep you away, the firemen piddle on the coal because they can't get out of the cab. It's piddled steam, firemen's piddled steam you've been playing in.' Although he had spoilt our lovely game for ever I had to laugh at Marjorie's refined disgust at Father using the word, 'piddle.' 'Fancy a father saying such a word to his daughters,' she said.

My mother would say, 'God wouldn't send a child into the world without a crust of bread,' and as she always said it wasn't the lustful man who had the children, when I was very young I assumed it was God who had sent Mother ten children. I felt that Father had some pleasure every time God decided to send another baby, but that Mother didn't, and I felt too that a man *must* have this pleasure but a mother *must not.* I knew after babies were born they belonged to the mother, and I thought mothers very lucky that the babies belonged to them and not the father, God only letting families have fathers to go out to work and get money for food. I knew God had been kind to my mother in giving her a husband who was not lustful, for if he had given her a lustful one, neither I nor my nine brothers or sisters would have been born. I had no idea what a lustful man was, but I knew from Mother's expression he wouldn't be a nice man.

I got the impression that butchers were lustful men. It was something which affected their hands through handling raw meat, for my mother was whispering with some aunts one day. They were talking about a butcher they had known in Beckenham whose wife, 'poor woman,' had to be ready for him every day when he came home to dinner. Since my mother always had my father's dinner ready for him every day and never made any fuss about it, I couldn't understand why she and my aunts were so sorry for the butcher's wife. Then she saw me listening and said, 'Little pitchers have big ears,' and they all stopped talking and looked at me as though I had been naughty.

'Watch your line of demarcation,' was another favourite saying of my father's, and we had no idea whatever of the meaning of this dreadful warning, although we knew it was very important. We had a vague idea of 'Look after your corner' and 'Take care of your clobber' and we well knew the meaning of 'You can't beat the old Aldershot oven.' This remark we all treated with contempt, including Mother, for she knew and we knew that it was not complimenting her on her lovely cooking. It seemed he would say this about the Aldershot oven after one of our best meals, so perhaps it was a compliment in a way and a tasty repast reminded him of his outdoor cooked meals. We didn't think it was a real oven, in fact we thought he was a bit crazy when he said it. But one Christmas we had an extra large goose which Mother hung from the top of the oven on a large hook. The goose kept falling down into the tin of fat and there seemed no way of suspending it. Father said he would make an Aldershot oven out in the back yard. Mother looked disgusted and frantically began to try and find other ways and means of cooking the goose before the military building was completed.

We all trooped out into the little yard where Father had assembled an odd assortment of stones and bricks. 'Phew,' said one of the boys, 'the cat's wee-wee'd on that one.' Father sent him indoors with a sharp rebuke that he was as obstinate as his mother, and my wicked brother went upstairs and stared viciously out of his bedroom window. Finally, after much swearing, Father lit an evil-smelling smoky fire under the bricks and we all ran coughing and spluttering and grumbling down into the scullery where Mother stood on guard with a triumphant look on her face. She had fixed the goose the other way up and it was sizzling merrily. Father was furious. He knew none of us would ever believe his Aldershot oven remark again. He himself had lost confidence in it, although he said if he'd had the proper tools and encouragement from the family, for once in his life, he could have cooked our goose as we'd never had it cooked before. He knew really it wasn't true, and as he went upstairs Mother said that when he'd made an Aldershot oven in the trenches in France and cooked 'the boys' a stew, he was the only one that ate it then. Father heard Mother's remarks and he said the trouble was that people were so used to artificial heating they couldn't recognise good healthy natural cooking when they saw it. It was the best goose we ever had, and although we knew Father could have eaten some more, out of pride he had to refuse it when Mother offered it to him. When I came downstairs that Christmas evening I saw Father at the meat safe picking a piece of goose. When he saw me he winked at me. I didn't tell Mother.

Father had been the bravest of soldiers, cheerfully suffering all manner of deprivations in the muddy Flanders trenches, but if he ever remarked on the days of the War (and he had his fiftieth birthday at Ypres), it was with humour. He had, however, one great and lasting fear, he could not bear the slightest breeze or air to blow on him and the terror and hate of his life was a draught. He felt the family all conspired against him by purposely leaving doors open. 'Shut that bloody door,' he seemed to be shouting non-stop in the winter, and he made Mother tut disapprovingly every time he shouted. Since the ten of us were in and out non-stop, never still, never closing the door, he was a swearing frantic man from autumn until spring and even in the summer he was still apprehensive at a cool breeze. He thought that people who lay in the sun were mad, and if we came home after a day out in the summer he would shout that we were all 'Non compus mentis' and then reiterate his way of life: 'I believe in moderation in all things,' he would say.

In the end, this man of inventions decided he would fit a spring to the kitchen door and for many months he seemed to be either standing on a chair or kneeling in homage at the kitchen door, getting many knocks as the family rushed in and out. The trouble was he could never get the spring to the correct springiness. Either Mother would be knocked backwards with a tray of food, or the younger ones had to call for aid to push the door open, or it would close so slowly that Father would be frustrated waiting for the final click, or it would close but not click and he would swearingly approach it and give it a mighty push. Then it would open again immediately for the unwelcome entry of another Cheggie.

Finally he put his awful glue-pot on the stove, ignoring our cries of 'Phew, what a stink,' and fixed old pieces of material all round the doors and windows. He made papier-mâché which turned into hard cement and pushed this everywhere, much to Mother's horror. No sooner had he left the house than every window and door was thrown wide open, for Mother loved fresh air as much as Father hated it. While cleaning she would, with the air of a defiant child, pick out of the door and window-frames much of his craftsman-made cement. Things lasted for ever with Father. He had so many false uppers and soles on his slippers and so many glued sheets and papiermâché fillings on his little shed that nothing of the original articles remained.

He could not bear waste, and when fire broke out in the rum quay at the West India Docks he went about for weeks like a broken man, shocked and horrified at the enormous catastrophe, almost snarling at us when we complained of the awful smell. The fire burnt for days, windows melted on houses some way from the docks and people came for miles around to view the fire; they seemed intoxicated by the fumes. Had any of the tourists seen my father they would have thought he had lost his nearest and dearest in the fire. Well, I suppose he had, for he had three sailor sons who received rum rations.

Father would say, 'Don't envy the rich man his wonderful food, for the rich man would envy the poor man's appetite.' The rich man couldn't enjoy his valuable possessions for they had to be locked away for fear of burglars. We need have no fear of burglars, we just had to place all twelve pairs of scuffed boots by the front door and a burglar would know he was wasting his time by entering.

Poor Father, we never listened to him. He often left the house saying, 'They are just like their mother, you can't talk to them.' I think we had closed minds, yet we all knew that our parents loved each other, possibly we didn't know it but were jealous of this love they bore for each other. We all wanted to be first and only in their eyes, and were always guiltily pleased when another member of the family was reprimanded.

My father was fanatical about the noise of cisterns, spending hours of his leisure time standing on the lavatory seat adjusting the ball-cock and valve (the cistern arrangements we refined ones called it), and listening when any member of the family left the lavatory, when out he would rush again. Mother said, 'He is a plumber and should know there is no such thing as a silent cistern.' I am sure with any encouragement my father could have invented one, but we were all so rough, he thought, in pulling chains. When we turned off any taps he would say, 'Don't forget, just finger and thumb, finger and thumb!'

According to the rest of the family and also public opinion, my father was a very handsome man, but I never thought so. I didn't like his waxed moustache; it would get wet when he drank his tea and he would suck it in before he wiped it on his handkerchief. He was very proud of his feet which were small and slender. He never had a corn or a callous or a misshapen toe or joint even after all the marching he had done in France and he would say that it was very important that we should always look after our feet. 'Never,' he would say, 'never wear second-hand shoes, ever.' I thought second-hand shoes would give one the fever by the way he said 'second-hand.' I thought of the boys I'd seen with no shoes at all and I wondered if we had been poor and I had no boots would I then be brave enough to wear a gift of second-hand boots.

2 A silver sixpence

My father was born Walter Chegwidden, in Crantock, a fishing village near Newquay in Cornwall where his grandfather kept a fleet of pleasure-steamers. The Chegwiddens lie in the church-yard and in the village stocks is a plaque to say that the last occupant was there for a record time because of the testimony of one Richard Chegwidden, who was my great uncle Cap'n Dick. He was the Captain who took Edward VII on a celebrated voyage so I knew he must be a first-class captain to be entrusted with the life of a king. Perhaps, after all, he wasn't a sneak and the man pilloried in the stocks was a real criminal.

I never felt my father had that sad feeling of nostalgic yearning for his birthplace as my mother did when telling of her lovely countryside. For one thing his father had despatched him to sea before the mast when he was very young and he said it was the worst period of his life. The harsh treatment meted out to the crew, the rancid food, the scurvy, all served to alienate him, and his father, untrue to type, left Crantock, and settled in Kent, where he founded a builder's business, training my father and each of his brothers in different aspects of the building trade. But when grandfather died my father was unable to control his brothers and it was difficult to get the rich customers to pay their bills. One couldn't be tough with the upper classes, and finally the failure of the business through bad debts caused long months of unemployment. Work was hard to get and there was no dole at that time; the end of the line was the Workhouse.

My parents had four small children then and came the day when they almost reached the end of the line, for Mother had sold all her bits of jewellery and furniture. Father was out tramping the countryside seeking any job he could get.

There was no food in the house, and Mother said she just fell on her knees and prayed. To keep her children happy and their minds off food she said they could help her tidy her work-basket, which didn't need such attention for she was always a band-box person. As she opened the basket, there on top was a shining silver sixpence. She bought six half-penny pieces of fish and two pounds of potatoes, and when Father returned tired and dejected from a fruitless search, there was an unexpected, delicious meal waiting for him. Mother just could not bear to sell his cricketing clothes for he was a fine cricketer, and she had them waiting for him as he was to play in a match at Mottingham that night. He was loath to go as he was near breaking-point, but she gently coaxed him into it. When he arrived at the Club House the Members had collected thirty shillings for him as he was so down on his luck, and a visiting player hearing that Father was a fully qualified plumber told him that Poplar Borough Council were in need of a good plumber.

Early the following morning Father set off for that un-known part of London and having obtained the job searched about to find accommodation and rented the little house, no. 3 Grove Villas. He sealed all the rooms and put sulphur candles in each one for he knew that houses in such areas were 'buggy,' and Mother moved from her nice clean sunny house in Beckenham with its large white scrubbed kitchen, to this cellar of a place in an almost foreign land. Years later she told me that although she kept it from my Father and the children, when she first set eyes on the house and the area she really thought her heart would break.

My mother's name was Leah. She was a very pretty woman, everyone said so, with auburn curly hair which she wore in a bun on the top of her head, but the little curls would not go straight so there was always a row of tiny curls across the top of her forehead. Her eyes were grey and she had a very straight nose, and a smiling mouth. She had small hips, was high-busted, and had small slender hands and feet. She was about five feet two inches tall, yet her mother had been nearly six feet tall and her father over six feet. I always thought Mother was short because she was one of twins. Mother had ten children and was always smiling, and her twin sister Emma had no children and was very serious.

Mother was one of thirteen children and her father worked as a carter at the Hall in Dinton, Wiltshire, where my mother was born. She said her father was a handsome man with dark curly hair and they had always thought their name was Mitchard – it was so in the family bible. But when his children went to school, for which he paid 6d. per week for each of them, the village schoolmistress and some local bigwigs decided that this was too high-flown for their station in life, and that they should be called Meatyard. When I was a little girl I was very angry at this for I thought Meatyard an ugly name, but Mother said, 'In those days, dear, we knew our place.'

I was glad when years and years later Somerset House could not trace her by the name of Meatyard when Father was applying for his pension. They wrote and asked if Mother had ever been known by any other name, and she was traced by Mitchard. Originally I think it had a 'de' in front of it, for Grandfather was supposed to have been a descendant of the Huguenots.

Her mother was a very houseproud and stern woman, but her father was more gentle. If he held a gentleman's horse for him or helped a visitor to the Hall he would sometimes be given 6d. and he would hurry straight home with it to Grandmother. Grandfather had a bible which was very old and very beautiful, and had the Apocrypha in it, in which he would enter all the children's births. The bible was read at every meal in Mother's house when she was young.

Nevertheless she was a bit of a rebel. The children had to curtsey to the squire even though he galloped past without acknowledging them, and spattered them with mud. One day Mother resolved not to curtsey to the squire and his lady when they rode by in their carriage and pair, and she walked on without 'bending the knee.' This act of rebellion so infuriated the squire's lady that she drove straight on to report

17

the incident, or rather non-incident, to the village school-mistress and the rector. Mother was punished for her dread-ful behaviour but, still defiant, at the next passing of the squire and his lady, she and her loyal brother made the most exaggerated of curtseys and bows, almost touching the ground with their heads. Their childish sarcasm and spirit was lost on the lady of the manor, for she appeared haughtily pleased.

One of my uncles gashed his hand very badly on a scythe. The squire sent him home to Grandmother to bind it up, so that he could return to work immediately. But it was too serious for Grandmother to attend to and she gave him money they could ill afford, and off he went to the doctor's, a five-mile walk away. The old doctor knew that his hand must be very badly gashed to need medical attention, and also knew that my uncle had walked five miles from his own village but he said, 'Show me your money before I look at your hand.' Mother's brother, with a touch of her spirit said, 'If thee'st woan't look first, thee'st woan't see it 't all,' and he walked the five miles home. Grandmother stayed up all night with him attending to his injured hand. He returned to work at dawn.

My Grandfather came up to the Great Exhibition of 1851 by stage coach and when old Lady Wyndham of the Hall died in London he had to bring her home by stage coach. My Mother said nobody knew she was dead, for she didn't look any different. The men had no time off from work, not even on Sundays, and Grandfather would get up at 4 a.m. to tend his cottage vegetable-plot to provide food for the family. At hay-making time all the children would help, and once Mother 'got at' the cider and she said it made her run backwards all the way home.

When my Grandfather was dying Mother was up in Lon-don and every day Grandfather asked for his 'smiling Leah' but she couldn't go because she had five small children and was very poor. He said if she didn't come by Wednesday it would be too late, and on Wednesday he died. Mother was broken-hearted for she loved her gentle father.

Mother, like the rest of the country girls, went into domestic service at an early age. At her first place in service, the lady of the house gave her one of her cast-off dresses. It was in a fine woollen checked material with tiny buttons from neck to waist, and had a high neck with real lace round it and velvet edgings. One day the house was burgled and Mother was required to attend court as a witness. She wore this dress, her only off-duty one, and in her hair she pinned a little lace rose she had made. The next day on the front page of the local paper was a full-length portrait of Mother with a report of the case. The judge complimented Mother on her elegant appearance, saying she brought sunshine into the court, giving her evidence in a most intelligent manner, and he felt that any employer having a servant like Mother would be proud of her. The next day Mother was summoned to the mistress's room and informed that she must never wear that frock outside the house again. She was to keep it to wear only in the tiny attic which she shared with the parlour maid.

She left shortly afterwards to work for the Greens, who were very fond of her. She was an exceptionally fine needlewoman and in addition to her duties as maid, her spare moments were spent on the mistress's clothes or the beautiful linen.

She loved the children of the house and they loved her. The little boy became Lord Green, Master of the Rolls, and my Father said he wasn't surprised, for whenever he met Mother in the park when the children were with her, the little boy would give him a judge's serious questioning gaze and make my father feel guilty for speaking to my mother. No followers were allowed; it was written in the 'domestic articles.' The same little boy knew my mother had a strong sense of humour and loved to make her laugh at the wrong times. If they had important people to dinner and she was called in to help the butler and the footman, he would try to catch her attention and do something to 'start her off.' Mother laughed at the time they had royal V.I.P.s to dinner, and young Master Green going into the dining-room to say good night to his parents said, 'Oh, I see you are using the best silver tonight, Papa.'

Mr Green was apparently a 'perfect gentleman' but extremely particular and fastidious. One evening the bell rang for Mother and she climbed the many flights of stairs only to find that Mr Green thought his bathmat wasn't quite straight. Another time he rang because his hairbrush wasn't level on his dressing-table – a very fidgetty man. His young wife, however, was just the opposite, happy-go-lucky and quite unfussy. One evening when Mother had known Father for a long time she became very brave and let him in through the kitchen door when the family would be safe at dinner. In her horror she saw young Mrs Green coming down the stairs to the kitchen, and Father was hurriedly pushed behind the sink curtain. Mrs Green hoisted her skirts for Mother to unlace her corsets, and Mother's hands shook with fear.

Once when the Greens were entertaining, the servants had been working like slaves from dawn and the butler sent Mother downstairs with the key to the wine cellar with instructions what to bring up if he rang. No one ever had the key to the wine cellar except the butler, and the other servants coaxed Mother to get them a bottle of very fine old port. The others persuaded Mother to have some and in a short time she was flushed and light-headed. The bell rang and she went up to the dining-room and by some miracle performed her duties properly, but after the guests had left, old Mrs Green the Master's mother who lived with them and managed the house, rang for Mother to go to her boudoir. 'Leah,' she said, 'I thought you uncommonly flushed tonight at table, I am going to give you some of my homeopathic medicine in case you are sickening for something,' and Mother had to drink a large dose of an obnoxious mixture in front of Mrs Green. This amused the other servants no end.

Mother had been with the family for many years and was earning £13 a year. She was so anxious to save up to get married that she did a thing unheard of in the servants' hall. She asked for a rise. Old Mrs Green was horrified and indignant as Mr Bumble was. 'Are you not happy here, Leah, you have a good home and situation, have you not?' Mother greatly daring and having burnt her boats said she thought

Mrs Green begrudged her the money she did pay, and left the room preparing in her mind to pack her clothes for she would surely be dismissed in disgrace. But much to the astonishment of the other servants Mrs Green gave her the rise she asked for.

We would listen as little children to the tales of 'the gentry,' of the enormous joints of meat and of the terrible waste of lovely food. The larders were bigger than our little house, and sometimes in the morning the huge vats of dripping would be wiped clean as though someone had washed them – rats, I thought. Then the gamekeeper would organise a rat hunt and all the men would take part. I wonder if Mother thought about this waste of food when years later, with a young family to feed, she was down to her last crust. I don't suppose so, for she always looked forward, never back. She never complained about her years in service, the long hauls upstairs with buckets of coal, the petty restrictions, and she never voted 'Labour' much to Father's disgust.

My parents were opposite personalities. He was a fiery socialist, banging the table while glaring at Mother and shouting, 'Better conditions for the workers, better conditions for the workers. Churchill robbed the road fund of sixty thousand pounds.' I thought that must be wrong. If my father knew it so did the police and Mr Churchill was not in prison. My mother infuriated my father for she wouldn't argue but would smile gently and he knew, however fierce he waxed, that she would remain a Conservative. 'Your mother's bloody obstinate and can't see further than the nose on her face,' he would scream, but still she wouldn't be drawn and he nearly choked when he thought of what Keir Hardie, Beatrice Webb and Ramsay Macdonald (well not so much him) had done for Mother and she was still disloyal to her class.

Father was selfish and sometimes uncouth, I thought, well a little, and I didn't like to see him arranging his truss when it became uncomfortable, although this was not to be wondered at for he had made it himself. It was an instrument of torture. An iron band sewn around with bits of padding and old shirts. Mother used to smile enigmatically and say, 'He only *thinks* he's ruptured,' but selfish as he was she was very proud of him, and his comfort and well-being were her chief concerns. She had nursed him through meningitis after he was concussed with a cricket-ball, and two bouts of pneumonia, and the doctor told father he owed his life 'to that wonderful lady, his wife.' The word 'lady' was I thought, such a lovely reward for Mother. She must have loved my father very much, I know, for she even washed and disinfected his spittoon, daily. No one else could have done that, and she always struggled to send him out with a shilling in his pocket for she said, 'A man must keep his pride.'

3 All present and correct

I was born in the house at no. 3 Grove Villas. It had, I always felt, an imposing address for that district, and could be advantageously deceiving for us, when it had to be given to people who did not know the district, for Poplar in the 1900s was in the heart of the East End slums.

This little house in 'The Grove' was one of about twenty-six. The first eight were very tiny and in pairs with a side door doing duty for the front, back and yard door. These eight 'elves' residences' were divided from the bigger bay-windowed houses by a very narrow side street called Arthur Street, and I always imagined that this street had been named after my eldest brother Arthur. Although I did not know what deed he had done to be so acclaimed, I was not surprised, for he was always so elegant in a 'I'll walk down the Avenue' kind of way. He had such an air of superior condescension with a 'Do I know you?' attitude to us younger ones that I was convinced that in that grown-up world of his he had done something very noble, or notable. The fact that he was half a century younger than Arthur Street made no impression on me, for if it hadn't originally been named after brother Arthur, then it had been renamed after him when he performed his mighty deed. I envied him this honour, and tried to pretend that something had been named after me. I chose 'A Dorothy Bag,' which was a very pretty velvet or silk bag all the young ladies carried.

A high railway wall ran down the whole length of 'The Grove' in front of the houses and my house also backed on to another very high building, the 'Poplar Public Baths and Wash-Houses,' so without neighbours at either front or back of us, the little house possessed a privacy unusual for that district.

Beyond the railway wall was the station and sidings where trains were shunted to and fro at dead of night. The noise rarely woke me but if it did I never found the clanking, squealing or crashing of the trucks as they collided with each other frightening or worrying, for that noise was the symphony which accompanied my birth. On the far side of the railway, set in pretty gardens, was the parish church of All Saints, our church, with its lovely clock and spire. From Mother's bedroom I could see the tops of the tall trees reaching up through the masses of little dwellings to pray to the sky, and, by climbing on to a chair, I could see beyond the church to the East India Docks where the ships had tall masts and coloured funnels painted with flags or stars. The sound of the shunting trains, the music of the church bells, the distant sirens of the ships, muffled like a throaty cough in foggy weather, were all a lovely and nostalgic part of my childhood.

The house contained four rooms. One of these rooms was really a cellar for it was half below ground level. It had a window, but as half of this was also 'underground,' from the street it appeared as though the occupants were a new race of 'torso' people. We lived, as it says in the hymn, 'looking ever upward to the sky,' for this 'cellar' basement we called the kitchen was the living, sitting, all-purpose room for twelve human beings. If I read about such a family and such a room in the newspaper today, I would be horrified and agree it was deprivation with a capital 'D,' but for us, through the magic of my mother, it wasn't like that at all. It was a room of great happiness and love, and we were all lively and 'normal.' (I think we were normal!) The fact that we were all 'present and correct' speaks volumes for her as a miracle-worker, for in any other family in that district in those circumstances the majority of us would have been natural or self-induced miscarriages or infant mortalities.

I never knew we were deprived. Things didn't worry us then. Towels, for instance, were often tails of the father's old working shirts hemmed round; sheets for beds, what were they? Some friends of mine drank out of jam-jars. Once when Marjorie had been ill in bed and a friend from her office was calling to see her, Mother cut an old sheet in two and placed one as an under sheet and the other half as a top sheet, and provided she didn't fidget, well then it was as good as a pair of sheets, was it not? Mother had her priorities right, children must have love and food, food for their growing bodies and love to make them secure, and plain food was always best for children, fortunately.

The window looked out on to a cement area which the local children called 'the airy.' The 'airy' had a small drain in it and I spent quite a lot of time sitting at the window dreaming that I could see red mice and blue mice running in and out of the drain. This kitchen, which was approached through the ground-floor bedroom, down a steep wooden staircase, contained a fireplace with an oven attached at the side, a stone copper with a little iron door in it and a heavy wooden lid on top, a coal cupboard with a sink in it, and at the end of the room a cream-painted dresser on which the crockery was kept. Behind a chintz curtain at floor level was a wide wooden shelf on which there were saucepans and cooking utensils, always called 'the pot board.'

This pot board had many valuable uses. It was our shelter during the Great War air raids, and our play-'room,' for it made a lovely cave or hiding-place, and at the far end near the coal cupboard Father kept his wooden chest containing his working 'tools.' He always kept the chest painted grey with beautifully picked out white letters on the side saying Sgt/Major W. Chegwidden, his regiment and number, and the two handles were made of thick plaited rope with little hairs sticking out which pricked through my dress if I sat against the handles whilst playing near the pot board. The chest was very heavy, and I thought my father must be the strongest man in the world, for he took it all the way to France with him, or so I thought. He kept his working boots next to the tool-chest and if ever there was a 'funny' smell in the kitchen these boots were always blamed and he was furious when he discovered 'someone' had placed them outside in the 'airy,' for they were often innocent. Once they were banished and the guilty party that time was the Stilton cheese an aunt had sent him from the country. Another time a nest of mice was found in the corner of the tool-chest.

Besides Mother and Father there were five sons and five daughters. Our parents had the top front bedroom, sharing this with the baby and the next youngest child. The girls had the top back bedroom and the boys the ground-floor bedroom. It was mostly two at the top and two at the bottom of a double bed and the odd one in a little truckle bed, the 'iron' bed we called that. The door to the kitchen stairs was in the boys' bedroom and we would all troop through that room on the way in, out, and up, on our various and many journeyings. A stranger in the boys' room would think we had risen from the bowels of the earth, for the kitchen stairs were so steep that, without a landing, we had to push the door of the room open before we reached the top stair.

Agnes was the eldest girl and Mother's first-born; I think perhaps she was also the most intelligent of the family. Mother kept a faded newspaper cutting and photograph of Agnes which hailed her as an infant prodigy at the age of three, when at a Charity Concert in Beckenham she acted and recited a poem, 'Miss Mouse Came to Tea.' I always felt fate was unkind to Agnes to start her off so well, then transport her to the slums and endow her with nine brothers and sisters. She was a pretty, sweet-natured girl with soft brown hair, melting brown eyes and a soft mouth, very easily moved to laughter or tears.

Winifred Beatrice, Mother's second daughter and her fourth child was never, for one moment, any worry; indeed she was more help than any of the family, Mother's support and unselfish stay. She had brown hair and eyes, a round Claudette Colbert type of face, a good figure, and a direct look, and she always 'whooped' when she laughed. Life for me, as a child, was full of Winnie and I just adored her, for she was so kind to Marjorie, the baby of the family, and me.

Winifred was brave and calm, so who else would 'Win the Scholarship' but her? The school was given a half-day holiday and her name went up on the Honours Board in gold lettering. She went to George Green's Grammar School for Girls, where the 'scholarship girls' were looked down upon by the paying pupils, but that didn't deter Winifred. She made friends with the most affluent and had the nerve to bring them home, where, strangely enough, they all seemed to want to come again.

Edith Amy, always known as Amy, was an entirely different person from Winifred in temperament as well as looks. She was petite with a mass of luxuriant dark hair and high cheek-bones, was very intense and dramatic, and possessed a quick temper. She was an exquisite needlewoman, had an unusual flair for clothes, and was a magnet for the opposite sex. My feeling towards her was one of caution because of her biting tongue, but I was envious of her conquests and her daring, for she was the first in everything. She had her lovely hair shorn before short hair was properly in, and she always started the fashions in Poplar. She had an actress's voice and would have us in tears at her recitations. She had the same girl-friend for years and years, and they would walk along, arm in arm, heads close together. I wondered what they talked about, for if I ever met them Amy would say in her Sarah Bernhardt voice, 'Go home, Dolly.'

I was Mother's ninth child and her fourth daughter and I detested my name, Dorothy, which was shortened to Dolly, I disliked my red hair, my largish nose, my thin legs and wished I had been born the only child of rich parents.

I was the one member of the family without a special gift, and the 'delicate one,' causing Mother worry and trouble. I was always 'gastric' and Mother would get different meals for me as she thought me a 'picky' eater and needed tempting. I always felt this special treatment meted out to me annoyed Amy, but I couldn't help feeling so ill. It would seem as though I was recalling some horrific dream, and calling for Mother I would faint. Once after I had been in bed for a long time with gastritis the doctor said he thought I was well enough to have solid food and he asked me if there was anything I felt I could eat. Pork chop was my first choice, sausages my second, fish and chips my third, and after this the doctor allowed me no more choices telling Mother I was to have a tiny piece of steamed fish, which I hated.

All the family loved little Marjorie, the baby, and they would say I was jealous of her from the moment she was born, although I cannot recall ever feeling like that, for I depended on her although she was three and a half years younger than me.

The memory of her birth is one of my earliest recollections. It was a warm day in September, close and humid, and I felt I wanted to be with Mother and not go out and play with Cecil. Agnes knew that the whole family must be got out of the little house somehow, and she asked Winnie to take all the children out for a walk. This was unusual, a walk on Sunday evening, and I didn't want to go but Agnes said, 'If you don't go, then Mother will have another baby and you won't be her baby any more.' In the end we all went down to Tunnel Gardens near Blackwall Tunnel, but it was closed and we all came home again. Agnes said to go out again and gave Winnie a penny to spend on us all. There were no shops open and, although Winnie was fourteen I don't think she knew at all what was happening. Anyway finally we came home and Agnes said to me, 'Mother has got something to show you.' I remember climbing the little wooden stairs. The evening sun was making strange shadows on the walls through the trees, and in Mother's bedroom the counterpane was very white – it was her best one. She was in bed although it wasn't bedtime and lying on her neck and sucking it was a baby. Mother looked pleased but somehow guilty and defiant, and I came out straight away without saying anything.

Mother's patience was infinite. She was not simple by any means although she had simple beliefs. She would say children are not really naughty, they are sick, tired, unhappy, bored, ill-treated or neglected, and a child's first need is love. She was the same with all children, not only her own ten, and all children loved her, for she found no fault with a child, but only in the way it was treated. Of Mother's love we all received one hundred per cent. She would never favour one more than the other, and would say regarding children, 'Never fish one and fowl the other.' But I always felt that Arthur, her second child, was a little special to Mother, and who could blame her if that was so, for of all ten of us, he was the one who really tried to rise above his surroundings.

He was always the 'perfect gentleman.' Any money he could scrape together when a boy he would spend on a new collar, etc. and even if his boots were as old as Charlie Chaplin's, they would have a shine on them one could see one's face in, and his trousers always had a knife crease in them. He would take such care of the little he had. He was a great help to Mother when Father was ill with pneumonia and looked after the younger ones and even one day made a beautiful stew. When he got the shopping he was very careful to 'watch the pennies' for Mother and make the best buy.

Charlie wasn't present during my childhood. He chose the life of a sailor quite early, later becoming a ship's plumber in the Merchant Service. He was Arthur's opposite in every way, Arthur was dark with a longish face, Charlie had red curly hair and was indeed 'rough and ready.' He hated collars and would buy cigarettes instead of personal adornments. Once Mother was in the little backyard when out of the top window came all Charlie's bedclothes, on fire. He was told, after that, not to smoke in the bedroom.

He very nearly spoilt Mother's record of rearing ten children, for when he was a baby he was once very ill, and dying with bronchitis. Mother's doctor in Beckenham who was always especially kind to her, came one evening and told her he had done all anyone could do for Charlie, it was just a question of time, a few hours, he thought. Father and her other two children were asleep and she said she never knew such a stillness to creep over the house. It was as though some silent invisible being was waiting. She cut out and sewed, through her tears, a little gown for Charlie, his shroud I suppose, sitting as close to the baby as possible, when there was a tap on the window and Mrs Holmes, her good neighbour, came to sit with Mother, and help her through the tragic hours. Suddenly Mrs Holmes said to Mother, 'If there is nothing anyone can do for the baby, we can do no more harm if we try a desperate remedy. Are you willing to try to give Charle some linseed oil?' Mother must have been in a terrible state, but she helped Mrs Holmes force this oil into the baby and they waited. They were sure they had hurried along his death and Mother sat Charlie upright on her lap and was crying all over his tiny red curls when he was suddenly and violently sick. The women thought he would never cease vomiting, but when the sickness finally ceased, he was breathing differently and on his upper lip Mother said there was a little bead of perspiration like a diamond. Mother bathed Charlie and put him in the little wooden rocking cot and he went to sleep quite peacefully. From that moment he started to recover. When the doctor came the next morning Mother said he was 'dumbfounded,' but the two women kept their desperate remedy to themselves.

David was Mother's only blond son, highly strung, but without Arthur's ambition. He would draw a capital letter and intertwine it beautifully with Grecian ladies, flowers, vases and ivy leaves. His technical drawing was perfect too. He excelled at chemistry and won a scholarship to Sir John Cass' School. But, lazy as the rest of us, as soon as father left for his club in the evenings, David would scoot out to play with his friends.

Leonard was a boy without malice, no one could quarrel with him, not even Arthur or Amy, and Leonard thought Amy the most fashionable and elegant female he ever knew. When he was young he seemed to hate actually leaving the premises. He would get to the front gate, and keep looking back, to see if we were looking for him still. He would make all sorts of funny faces to amuse us and we would laugh, but the older ones would say, 'Mother, come and look at Len acting silly at the front gate.' They were disgusted, but Mother would smile and say, 'Take no notice of him, he'll tire before you do. He only does it because he knows you are watching.'

Cecil was the fifth and last boy and two years older than me. He and I were so much alike in appearance that we could have been taken for identical twins, and I hated that. What girl wants to be likened to a boy? He was easy to get on with and although Mother tried to put him in an office, he went and joined the Royal Navy one day, much to her sorrow. To be fair to him, in those days firms would employ boys at fourteen, then when at sixteen they would be called upon to pay National Health contributions for the lads, they would then sack them and employ other boys of fourteen.

We made up our own games and never missed not having toys. The boys played 'Barbers,' and I was always the one to have my hair cut or even be shaved. I was always the prisoner in the 'Wars.' We played 'Sewers,' and turned all the kitchen chairs upside down for the steps, obviously we didn't really know what sewers were, for I am sure we wouldn't have squelched and splashed about so happily. We once played a very energetic game and knocked clothes which had been ironed and were airing on to the fire. Mother almost jumped down the stairs at our awful screams and after she put the fire out she put her arms round us and kissed us, so relieved we were safe. Many mothers in that district would have 'bashed' the kids for being careless and for the terrible loss of the clothes.

Cecil was an extra lively boy: when he wasn't climbing or leaping from chair to table he was playing with the fire. He would get bits of string, light them and watch with fascination as they burnt slowly away. While Father was at work one day Cecil did that forbidden thing and opened Father's toolchest. Rummaging about amongst the tools and bits of lead and copper piping he came across what we thought was the metal end of a pencil. Cecil rushed with his find to the fire and placed it amongst the red coals, pushing it down with the end of a steel poker which always hung on a hook by the oven. Suddenly there was a blinding flash, an almighty bang, and a live bullet exploded from the fire across the room towards Winifred, who by some lucky chance was standing in an athletic attitude with her legs astride cleaning the dresser. The bullet went right through her skirt and embedded itself in the wooden dresser. We were all very shaken and quiet when Mother returned from shopping. She was angry that Cecil had been disobedient and opened the tool-chest, and furious that Father had left it unlocked, but said that miracles do happen, for it was a chance in a million that it missed all us little ones in such a small space. She said that if Cecil ever played with the fire again, unhappy though she would be, she would have to burn him so that he would know what fire was really like. Of course we all cried; we didn't want Cecil to be burnt and Mother wouldn't be Mother then for she never hurt any of us, not even with a slap, but we cried anyway for she never broke her word. We needn't have worried for the bullet was Cecil's swan-song and he lost interest in the fire from then on. Nobody ever told Winifred after that incident to stand in a more ladylike posture.

Grove Villas was a short cut to the main road from the Docks and Shipping Offices and I would stand at the gate of the little house at tea-time watching the business people pass on their way to the railway station. The 'bosses' with their shiny leather attache cases, newspapers under their arms, the Lascars from the ships, sometimes a drunken seaman, the workmen in their blue dungarees, like Father, and always, without fail, the 'swearing' man. He was a big man, red-faced, going bald, he would always charge quickly along, then suddenly stand still and shout in a loud voice a whole string of swear words and sayings, twitching all the time, then peaceful again he would start charging on his way. People averted their eyes and pretended not to notice him, and I would copy them. My brothers said he was 'shell-shocked.' I didn't know what they meant but felt satisfied at this statement. Some-times one of the 'bosses' would rumple my hair with his newspaper and I would smile shyly and feel very honoured.

I was not afraid of the 'swearing' man for I always knew that down in the kitchen behind me would be Mother. I often waved, for I could see the top of her head and her eyes above the 'airy' wall. Mother, without fail, was always there when I needed her. Once she was lying at the bottom of the wooden steps, not moving, and looked different somehow, but even then when I patted her face and called she opened her eyes and smiled, and when she got up my eldest sister came and gave her a glass of water.

4 Down Chrisp Street

Poplar's market-place, Chrisp Street, 'Cristreet' as we locals called it, a stone's throw from where I lived, was a second home to me, a long wide road stretching from Poplar to Bromley-by-Bow, a lively, happy thoroughfare full of exciting stalls and people. It didn't matter that I had no money to spend, there was so much to see and to listen to. On Saturdays there was always one member of the Chegwidden family to be found 'down Cristreet.'

I would go shopping with Mother to help her carry her heavy bags but then she would say they were much too heavy for my young arms, so I was no help to her really. I would get bored standing and listening while she chatted with friends, for Chrisp Street was the only social outlet mothers had.

The large, off-white, imposing building on the corner, half in Chrisp Street and half in East India Dock Road, was THE BANK where Winifred's friends the Logan girls lived, their father being the bank manager, and it was one of my ambitions to prove to my friends that my older sister moved in a high social sphere. For us it was like associating with royalty, and I always gazed up at the barred windows on the second floor of the bank in case Winifred was there and might look out of the window to amaze my friends and bathe me in reflected glory. But Winifred never came to the window, and so it was always, 'Oh, Dolly Chegwidden, you do tell 'em,' from my friends. In other words, not only did they know me for a liar, but I was always trying to make them believe my sister was superior to their sisters, and of course friends don't do this, not real friends. They were content with things as they were and I knew I was content too, but it didn't stop that feeling of worship, or was it envy, when I saw the girls from the bank or the vicarage. Some of them went to boarding-school, which I thought must be paradise. School for twenty-four hours a day! My friends thought me crackers when I said I'd like to be a teacher. It may be cowlike to be contented, but unfulfilled ambitions are torture to those who suffer them, and my friends were quite happy with their lot and thought themselves lucky not to be barmy, 'Like what Dolly Chegwidden is.'

Outside the bank was Burgess's large fruit and vegetable stall. They were there all the years I can remember and knew our family well. Mother said, 'Mrs Burgess is such a nice respectable woman.' Her sons all helped on the stall which was lit at night by huge naphtha flares which hissed and spluttered and turned lovely colours, yellow, orange, red and blue. The fruit was all shiny and polished and the vegetables always fresh. Mother only really bought fruit at Christmas time, but Mrs Burgess would save some specked fruit in a box under the stall for when Mother was in funds. At Christmas time the fruit we bought was as large and shiny as the fruit on display. Sometimes in the summer we had a hopping apple, which was a very large green cooking apple, brought home by neighbours from the hopfields. It was sweet and crisp to eat and Mother would share it between the young ones. Cabbage was the mainstay of our diet and considered to be very important and necessary to the family, but I would never eat it and Mother never forced me, thinking she might put me off for ever.

Near the bank was the eel shop and next to the eel shop was the Star in the East, a public house with patterned glass windows on which the name was engraved in the glass. People would stand outside with jellied eels and beer and spit the eel bones on to the pavement. I hated the smell of the eel shop, the parsley sauce, vinegar, and bodies. The windows were always steamed up and inside were scrubbed white benches and thick china bowls in which the customers had their hot eels and mashed potatoes and 'liquor'; this liquor was the parsley sauce. The vinegar bottles didn't pour like ours at home and had to be shaken violently, so if you weren't used to them you could shake vinegar over everyone. The floor was covered with a thick layer of sawdust and outside were zinc trays in which masses of grey and black slimy eels writhed, intertwined, waiting for a huge bloody red wet hand to grab one up, slit its throat or belly, and then chop its head off. The eel still wriggled when it was in little pieces only joined to itself by skin, and my brother said the eel wouldn't die until sunset. I used to wonder how each piece of eel knew the other pieces were still alive, and how the head, which was in a pail in another place, could tell his pieces when it was sunset. I thought eel-eaters must be like cannibals. My family and friends all liked eels.

There were two attractive shops, Konskiers, and Silverblatts where Amy, who was seven years older than me, bought pretty underclothes and 'bust bodices'; and some Jewish fashion shops with chic hats, coats and frocks; and Neaves, a huge open-fronted credit drapers with hundreds of pairs of heavy hob-nailed boots hanging so low on string that men would have to duck to get inside, otherwise they'd get a nasty knock. Inside were piles and piles of striped flannelette working shirts, without collars. The assistants wore brown overalls so it wasn't posh and I thought it the dullest shop in the world. Women would take a dog-eared torn book to Neaves and pay 6d. per week to get clothes on credit.

Between the regular stalls, where the stall-holders were as well known to us as the shop-keepers, were wide spaces where travelling pedlars sold their goods from the ground. It was exciting to see the different foreign people there each week for they had a lively patter, some very comical, all fluent. There was the gipsy with large golden ear-rings and golden sovereigns stitched round her brightly coloured head-scarf. She had a dozen beautifully coloured love birds and if anyone paid her, usually a young man or woman, she would put out a little stick towards one of the birds and it would fly down, forage among a box of small coloured paper squares and bring out a 'fortune.' Near the gipsy was the man in the frock coat and top hat. He sold medicine which was magical, for it cured every illness known to mankind (and some not yet discovered). Warts, loss of hair, influenza, gout, intimate ailments. I had no idea what an intimate ailment was, yet I knew it was a disease which must not be enquired about from grown-ups. My brother Cecil said of this magical medicine, 'It polishes your boots lovely.' The medicine man would talk non-stop about all the places in the world where he had cured people after doctors had given them up; even royalty, abroad of course, were in his debt. He had his own special bottle of medicine from which he drank from time to time, and this he kept in his pocket. His pitch was on the corner of Kirby Street where the Salvation Army band would play on Saturday nights, and when the cymbals clashed and the band started up, he would say, 'Oh, Jesus, what a holy row,' but he still went on talking non-stop and I was sure he could never be silent. I wondered if he was married and what it was like at home for his children. Obviously none of them would ever be ill with free magic medicine, but I thought they might be dumb for they would never get a chance to speak while he was there.

Further down was the man in irons and chains. My brother said he was Houdini's cousin. He was short, ever so strong-looking and was always stripped to the waist, sunburnt and covered with tattoos, flowers, birds, butterflies and words. Across his chest, and back, and round again towards his neck was a huge serpent, tattooed in red and blue. As the man moved, the snake writhed as though it were real and its long fangs stretched upward towards his throat. I had to put my head almost upside down to see some of the tattoos the right way. People paid money to see Houdini's cousin escape from the chains and iron bands. One day I saw him being chased by a policeman, who just lifted the chains off the chain man, so then I knew that policemen were very strong, for I never saw anyone in the crowd ever get the chains off.

I went to Sukey's stall for a ha'porth of pot-herbs, and it was good value, for Mother said it was enough to flavour her stew or rabbit. Sukey was lovely, in a snow-white overall, the happiest and fattest woman I had ever seen. I always thought she was sitting down at the little table-stall and it came as a real shock when I grew older to realise she had been standing up all the years of my childhood and that she was her own human arm-chair. Next to Sukey was the rabbit woman. Mother would get a wild rabbit for sixpence. Of course she needed two for our family, but when Father's pay increased to £2 a week, later on she would sometimes have an Ostend rabbit. Mother never liked to see the eyes of a rabbit, they used to make her feel sad, and I thought she was remembering them running about in the meadows when she was young.

Agnes would sometimes get the dinner for Mother. Mother would give her sixpence and she would buy half a pound of leg of beef, a ha'porth of pot-herbs, a pennyworth of suet, and three ha'porth of potatoes, and for this sixpence there was a dinner for all. I suppose the young ones had gravy and dumplings. Mother used Edwards' dessicated soup powder (it wasn't powder really) which she thought 'made' the stew. There was, of course, her big rice pudding to follow. Sometimes she would buy an enormous cod's head for a penny. (Such a lovely lot of fish left on the head!) We had stews mostly, but sometimes on Sunday for 2s. she would buy an 'oven breaker,' which was the large back ribs of meat, and she would do it very slowly in the oven. Often, herself, she had a 'kettle bender' which was a cup of crusts with hot water, pepper and salt, and a knob of margarine. She said it was like broth and she always had this meal before Father came in for his.

I used to love watching her pack Father's lunch. He would have a huge Cornish pasty which he called 'Man Friday's Footprint' and a tea parcel. She would take several thicknesses of newspaper, fold them, and in the middle shake a mound of sugar, then on top of this some tea from the caddy, followed by another layer of sugar; on top of this again would be poured a thick river of creamy Nestle's milk and then more layers of sugar and tea. Father would boil it all up in a billy-can and he loved it. Sometimes for tea he would have a large plate of toasted cheese. I would watch him put vinegar and pepper on it, and it looked like nectar to me, but I never had any. Mother said it would give me the nightmares and of course nobody in his right mind would want the nightmares.

Once, for a special treat, Mother bought some little cabinet puddings from the coffee shop across the road where my brother Arthur's friends lived, and the little individual puddings in their tiny basins caused great fun. Black treacle was very good for us, Father said, and we had it on Mother's huge suet puddings. My brother Leonard always had to have the pudding cloth, for he was always afraid some of the pudding near the string, where the cloth became creased, would be wasted.

Mother would tell me that when she was first married she would buy a large leg of mutton for 2s. 6d. She always bought white cheese but my friends' mothers bought red cheese. She would buy Sunlight soap for washing the clothes, but John Knight's Family Health for washing us. She always tried to buy a small amount of butter for me, because I was delicate, and for herself, because she would sometimes make her main meal of bread and butter. Neither she nor I liked jam, and with jam or treacle you just couldn't taste the margarine.

Oxenham's of Chrisp Street was a grand emporium and on very special occasions Mother would buy hair-ribbon for my younger sister, Marjorie, and me. Mine was always crushed strawberry and Marjorie's blue. Mother would lovingly stroke my ribbon with her finger and say, 'Crushed strawberry is *the* colour for Dolly.' But since I had reddish curly hair I didn't fancy the crushed strawberry colour and sometimes if I wanted to annoy Mother I would call it pink; she always answered, 'No, dear, it isn't pink, it really is crushed strawberry.' Since I'd never had strawberries it meant nothing to me. I hated pink. We would be given a packet of pins for a farthing change; the packet was green and each pin was in its own little hole. The assistant on the ribbon counter suffered from a head complaint and I would wonder on my way to Oxenham's whether she would have short curly hair, bald patches with tufts, or if she would be wearing a mob-cap. If she was wearing a mob-cap it would mean she had no hair at all, then I thought she would look like the picture on the map of the man further along Chrisp Street who talked without stopping for breath. He held a baton in his hand and kept pointing to a head on a map. The head was like the countries in my brother David's atlas which he brought home from school for homework, for it had lines and rivers all over. On the ground in front of the man was a scarlet plush chair with a gold cord across the front of it. My brother said, 'He tells your bumps,' and I thought the cord across the chair was to stop someone falling on to the ground with fright if the man told that person's bumps something nasty.

When we reached the financial stage of sometimes having the Ostend rabbit instead of wild rabbit, then Coppins the butcher's was a port of call for he sold English meat, not 'catmag.' Old Mr Coppins treated Mother like a lady and she would laugh with him, but I thought he was a most frightening bad-tempered man. He would go berserk if a woman poked her finger in any of his meat and bring his chopper down hard, just missing the poking finger with its black-edged nail. When I went to his shop for Mother by myself I would stay right back against the wall because of his down-coming chopper and be very glad to leave his shop, for he was always red-faced and swearing.

The one chemist in Chrisp Street was Tucks but I only went there once, for he gave me my medicine in a large green liniment bottle. When at Mother's insistence I had finished the last dose, out fell a piece of sticky paper. To our horror attached to this horrible brown paper was an enormous blue-bottle. My father said I could have been arsenicked, poisoned. We always went to Abelsons further away in the main East India Dock Road. He was a very charming, very polite

Jewish gentleman with thick pebble glasses, very guttural and adenoidish. We would wait excitedly for, on completion of our business, he would say, 'And ith there anythig elth?' and this never failed to amuse us.

Winifred was always losing her money in Chrisp Street for she went shopping with a note folded very small in the palm of her hand and when she went to pay for her goods would find she had no money. She would retrace her steps and nearly always found the note, for she had made it look like a tiny piece of thrown-away paper.

On Saturday nights the Jewish man on his sweet stall was a music-hall turn. He had the patter of an Alfred Marks of that day. He would gather up whipped cream walnuts, candy and toffee and sell them all in one parcel amid screams of laughter, but everyone waited for the punch line. On one side of the sweet man was the large flower lady, enormously breasted, bright-faced, with arms red from being in and out of pails of water. She made wreaths for funerals. On the other side of Sweet Harry was a gentle blind man. With eyelids closed he would sell matches and bootlaces from a little tray suspended round his neck. He always wore a bowler hat and every few seconds he would say gently, 'Is there anyone else, is there anyone else?' Sweet Harry with perfect timing would tell the crowd, 'Last night the flower woman was in bed and she said . . .' and then came the blind man's, 'Is there anyone else, is there anyone else?'

Clarkes the grocers would put a stall outside the shop on Saturday nights with bargains. My father said, 'Rubbish the manager wants to get rid of,' and this stall was managed by an eager, tiny, blond boy who would call out in a piping voice, 'Ladies, get your woocherchooster sauce here.' I thought him very stupid not to be able to say Worcestershire properly. One day a woman knocked a bottle of sauce on to the ground and as the brown liquid ran out I was struck by the look of sheer terror on the little boy's face.

There was nothing one could not buy in Chrisp Street if one was rich, everybody was so happy and jolly and all the shop assistants seemed to vie with each other to serve a customer. 'The trouble with Chrisp Street,' Mother would say, 'it is impossible to send Dolly on an errand, she dreams her time away.' The whizzing canisters containing money and bills shooting in all directions above one's head in Oxenham's, the barrel organ outside the public house, the man playing the violin with his eyes closed, the Indian man with his head and legs all bound round with cloth, the hot faggots, the black puddings and pease pudding, the noise, the smell, the music and, oh, the life!

5 A lovely place to live

I loved Poplar, its people, its places, its atmosphere; it was the only thing I was ever brave enough to defend. Years later, when I was working in the City with 'pin money' girls from Kensington, Wimbledon and St John's Wood, and it was discovered I came from Poplar, I felt they almost drew away from me physically as though I were a refugee from a leper colony. 'Oh,' they would say, horrified, 'Poplar, isn't that in the sl—s?' or, 'That's where the poor come from, the down and outs, isn't it?' 'How terrible it must be for you to live in such a filthy place.'

But Poplar, to my mind, was a lovely district, for it contained all that anyone could need. Beautiful churches, schools, parks, a library, hospital, docks, a pier, public baths and even a swimming-bath. We had a nautical college and a bookshop famous all over London.

It wasn't necessary for one to be able to read to know, even from a long way off, what goods some shops sold, for many of the shops had, outside, very large and exciting signs of their trade. The barber had a long pink and white striped pole and Father said it was something to do with blood-letting in the olden days. The ironmongers had an enormous key, the butcher a picture of a ferocious well-fed bull, one shop had an enormous pink teapot aloft on the roof and this shop, a grocers, was always known as Teapot Jones. The shop which sold clothes to seamen displayed an enormous thigh-length boot, and I used to tell Marjorie it was a seven-league boot of a giant. But the sign I thought must have cost a lot of money was outside the Pawnbrokers' shop which was called the Pledge Office – three golden balls. I thought they were solid gold for the sun was always shining on them when I went out in the morning.

On Monday mornings there was always a queue of women standing close together waiting for the Office to open, bundles under their arms and the boys would call out, 'Same as last week, shift and drawers ninepence,' but the women took no notice. Mother wasn't a Monday morning regular and indeed she never had the courage to go herself, but always sent two members of the family. Of course, Father mustn't know, and no other fathers seemed to know of their wives' and children's visits to this establishment. So the suit, or whatever, was camouflaged and the children like adventurous spies always keeping a watchful eye open for an unexpected father. We were rich, for Mother wrapped Father's suit in a sheet of brown paper which was put away very carefully each week. A friend of mine was very envious of this sheet of brown paper for she had to take the clothes to be pawned in an old piece of shirt, but once she managed to save a penny and she bought a sheet of brown paper. This was her most cherished possession for the years of her childhood and each week she ironed this so that it always looked new, and each week she regained her pride and felt she could look the world in the face. I wondered where people thought my friend took this large brown paper parcel each week. It couldn't be the Post Office for she came home with it on Saturdays and the postman always delivered. But this penny sheet of brown paper made my friend very very happy. She was a very serious girl, extremely capable, and took her pawnbroking visits very seriously. On Mondays, in the winter, she would take her father's watch. This family heirloom was only pawned in the winter for then her father arose in the dark and went to bed in the dark so he didn't see that the watch was missing. Her mother warned her not to let the pawnbroker put the watch too heavily on the counter. My friend would watch him very closely, her hand at the ready, and always, when I was with her, she was quicker than the pawnbroker, and the watch always had the cushion of her hand for safety.

Mo Finer, the Jewish dentist, had a surgery in East India Dock Road. He was a large brutal-looking man with a red face and thick lips. He always appeared to be eating and wiping his mouth on a grubby white overall. He pulled teeth free if the victim was willing to sit in the window for a public extraction, a novel if noisy way of advertising. If you were a coward then you would have to pay to have your tooth removed behind closed doors. So one had a choice, unless of course you were a penniless coward, then you were in for a bad time, for I believe Mo removed teeth free without anaesthetics of any kind. My brothers said Mo could pull a man across the road by his teeth, he was so strong. As he pulled teeth he would throw them out into the road. We never went to Mo Finer. When I became of school age I had my teeth removed by the clinic and I thought it was heavenly. Under gas I really did see the rabbit running round and round as the dentist had promised I would, and I just longed to have gas again. The dentist said I was his best patient and the first one ever to rush into the surgery and jump eagerly into the swivel-chair.

The public baths and wash-houses backed on to our house and from the wash-house came an everlasting hot, soapy, steamy aroma. The door of the wash-house was always open and in the dark interior one could catch a glimpse of red wet-faced women in sacking aprons and men's boots doing their weekly wash, or a daily wash if they took in washing for a few shillings. The clothes would dry in a very hot open oven suspended on iron rails on metal wheels. The noise of these metal wheels was deafening and the women would have to shout all day to be heard above the noise. Inside the wash-house they looked like Amazons with their sleeves rolled up above their soapy elbows, but when they came out and packed their prams with sacking-covered washing they looked old. With rusty black hats, or a man's cap fixed flat with a large bead ended hat-pin on top of their scragged hair, they seemed very small and bent. They would have to hold the large bundle of washing with one hand and push the go-cart with the other. Their ankles seemed to be bent over and their shoes never looked as though they belonged to them.

When we were too old for Mother to bathe us in the little tin bath, we would join the older ones every Friday and go to the public baths. We would have to go early for a large crowd collected in the waiting-room when the young people came home from work. It was impossible for a girl to pop into the baths before a dance, etc. for sometimes it was necessary to wait over two hours for one's bath. We always took a book to read, and always saw the local brides there the night before their wedding. I never had a satisfactory bath there for I was always nervous of authority, and as I could never be sure whether the water was the right heat when I tried it with my hands at the attendant's request, I had a bath either too cold or too hot and often came home looking like a lobster. I could never pluck up courage, as the others did, to call out, 'More hot, or cold, in number . . . please,' even though the baths rang with the sound of such requests. When the attendant said, 'Hurry along in number . . . please,' I thought how brave the girl in that numbered bath was, to have to be asked to hurry. I wished I could just lie in the warm water with no one outside waiting for the bath. One Friday evening I was at the baths with Winifred when a neighbour's daughter came out. She was an anaemic copy of Mary Pickford, very thin, with bent ankles on high-heeled patent shoes. She wore a moth-eaten fur and said to Winnie, 'Oh I feel a ton lighter now,' and Winnie remarked to me she wasn't surprised for that was the young lady's yearly visit. Poor frail little thing, she just wanted to look like a film star, and she was so thin I should think it would have been dangerous for her to visit the baths each week.

Next to the baths was the blacksmiths and I used to love to watch him shoe the horses. He was only a little man but he had huge forearms. I wondered why the horses didn't cry out in pain when he put the hot sizzling shoe on the hoof. Mother said she always knew when I had watched the horses being shod for I smelt of stables. The gutters in my childhood were always filled with chaff from the horses' nose-bags.

We went to the 'pictures' on Saturday mornings. The Picture Palace was like a huge garage with dirty red doors opposite Mrs Crutchington's shop and it cost a ha'penny. It was called the Star Picture Palace and we would all cheer when the pictures finally started for the screen was a long time flickering and shaking and tearing itself in two with brief glimpses of the previous week's serial before it settled down, and whenever it broke down during the performance, which was often, we would all boo loudly. A lady played the piano, sad music, frightening music, and happy music according to how the film was progressing and what was taking place. Because we had so few 'arrants' to do, we were nearly always the first ones there and so sat in the front row where the cowboys were nine feet tall, the horses hunched up in the middle and the heroine had a 'Dish ran away with the spoon' face.

Marjorie was the most terrible person to accompany to the pictures. Even when she was older she didn't improve much. We all left the world mentally, but she left it physically as well in a sense. When the heroine was tied to the railway line, and tried to fight her captors, Marjorie would fight in her seat. When the poor mother was pleading with the wicked landlord for her starving children, Marjorie was on her knees pleading too. Her screams of terror when the heroine was about to be tortured seemed louder to me than the frightening music being played by the lady pianist and I would thump Marjorie to bring her back to the world. All in vain, she never felt or heard me, and I ceased going to the pictures on Saturdays long before Marjorie did, for she could wait patiently until the next episode of an exciting serial. Rather than wait and wonder, I decided not to go. I hated serials, I just had to see a complete picture, and most of the films shown to the children had been cut and made into serials, for by chopping the films into little bits they would last the Picture Palace for weeks and weeks. I always thought it had been raining on the screen and it wasn't until years later I realised it was the poor quality of the film. The black streaks moved everlastingly up and down.

Saturday was disinfectant day, too. The 'disinfecting' the children called the white cloudy liquid which was supplied free by the council provided the requisite number of bottles was taken each Saturday morning. We had to be very careful not to spill any for my brother Cecil had warned us, when passing the job over to Marjorie and me, that it 'rots your boots,' and being clever I knew that once it had rotted my boots then it would start on my feet. Father used the disinfectant for cleaning the drains which he did with great vigour as though he was attacking the devil. All the time he would talk about the ignorant people who turned up their noses because they thought free disinfectant was charity and if they took advantage of it people would think they were accepting charity and were also dirty. Disinfectant from the borough was for the dirty poor most people thought, but I knew we were sensible for Father said it was lovely stuff. I have seen him pour it over a cut finger and it would heal in no time. Mother said some women put it in their wash to make their clothes look white, but Mother said hers were white through proper washing. We all have our standards.

High Street, Poplar, on a Saturday morning was a human ant colony, a never-ending stream of children hurrying along, or having a rest, with clinking bottles. Well, we hurried one way when the bottles were empty, on the way back we carried the bags in different positions to relieve the strain on our arms.

The disinfectant depot was not the 'dust instructor.' The dust instructor was where the dustmen took the rubbish; it was really the dust destructor, but everybody called it instructor. The disinfectant depot was past the Nautical College, a beautiful white building, in the High Street. We turned into a steep cobble-stoned yard where all the children had to start running – it was well known that no one could walk down that slope. We had all tried. In winter it was extremely treacherous and we were thankful it was on the way in when we were carrying empty bottles for if we had slipped on the way out we might have been rotted all over. Sitting in the depot at an enormous dark green carboy was a man with a grey cap, a silent man who never spoke, but just held out his hands for our empty bottles. We always said 'Thank you,' for Mother reminded us every Saturday about doing this. The large cork of his carboy was pure white and spongy where the disinfectant had touched it. That was proof Cecil spoke the truth.

The workhouse was attached to the depot and across the

yard we could see through barred windows little men in coarse grey suits and caps going to and fro and yellow-faced vacant-looking old women staring at us. I knew the workhouse was a sad place because my brother David would recite a poem about Christmas Day in ' IT.' I always took this poem very seriously.

One Saturday morning on the way back from the Depot we rested outside Coldstreamer's, the grubby little general shop with stairs up to the glass door which was plastered with advertisements for Mazawattee tea and Edwards' 'dessicated.' I was very fond of the Mazawattee tea advertisement for my maternal grandmother had won ten shillings per week for life for submitting a winning couplet to them. Ten shillings per week for life in 1900 was a fortune. Mother never shopped at Coldstreamer's, secretly thinking it a gossip shop where lots of women collected. Mother never gossiped or said anything unkind about anyone. Mrs Coldstreamer had a lemon-shaped face, lemon-coloured hair and she possessed a lemon-coloured cat, a huge beast. In the dark little window were displayed black bowls filled with butter beans, rice, sugar, etc. all very dusty and ancient-looking.

On this Saturday morning as we rested with our burdens, into the shop window climbed the huge lemon Tom. I could see Marjorie's indignation beginning to take on its righteous role, 'Look at that Tom,' she said, 'he shouldn't be near food.' Tom sniffed at every bowl in turn, then when Marjorie was worried he would lick the beans or the rice, or even the prunes, he turned to the brown sugar and to Marjorie's choking horror, he slowly lifted one leg, looked straight through the window at Marjorie and defiantly soaked the brown sugar which I noticed did not change colour. I suspected he had done that trick before, hence the sniffing. Marjorie said she must tell Mrs C. who would be so pleased to know. Whatever emotion that good lady would feel, with a shopful of customers, I knew it would not be pleasure and I tried to dissuade Marjorie by saying that there was nothing to worry about for our mother didn't buy anything there. My 'it's all right for us,' attitude made Marjorie turn on me.

'There's other people, you know, Dolly,' she said. She went up the steps and as the bell rang as she opened the door I thought discretion was the better part of valour and ran home to tell Mother what Marjorie was doing. When Marjorie arrived home she was seething. It seemed her reception from Mrs C. was not as she had imagined it to be, no grateful thanks, but extremely short shrift. Apparently she said to Mrs C., 'You will be pleased with me for telling you, Mrs Coldstreamer, that your Tom cat has just wee-weed in the brown sugar in the window.' That good lady replied, 'Well, why would it worry you, your mother will never buy it.' It was Marjorie's first lesson that virtue is not its own reward.

There was always the street to play in, lovely Bath Street, for there was nowhere to play in The Grove. On Saturday afternoons and after school we would always ask if we could go out to play. Our friends were always there before us for they took their thick slice of bread into the street to eat. Mother made us sit at the table all together to eat our tea and she sat down too at the top of the table behind her huge brown teapot. She would say, 'Don't talk to any strange men, and come in when the church bell rings.' The church bell chimed for the hours but we knew she meant the evensong bell at 7-30 and without fail at the first evensong peal we would be away home as Mother had told us to.

We took with us pieces of rope for skipping, but sometimes one girl would have an enormous thick tarred length of rope which stretched right across the road, then it was a mass effort, boys as well. The boys looked very awkward and could not skip like the girls. 'Allee in together girls, never mind the weather girls,' we would chant. The first one in under the heavy swinging rope had to be very durable with extra long legs for it was some time before everybody was in and skipping, and if your legs turned weak the rope would give them a nasty bruise. The two children turning the heavy rope had to be Amazons too and woe betide them if they let the rope droop and so caused us to be out through no fault of our own.

Sometimes we would have a grotto season. Someone would

build the first grotto and then on every street corner a grotto would arise. The older girls, Winifred and Amy did quite well out of their grottos, Winnie calm and business-like, Amy small and artistic. Marjorie and I were afraid to participate in our friends' grottos for Mother was against what she thought was begging. 'Nothing but charity,' she would say, 'Never let anyone know you are poor. There is nothing to be ashamed of in being poor, it's the pleading of poverty which is so shaming.' Winifred and Amy were more daring – how they hid their ill-gotten gains I don't know. In the end, of course, they were found out.

The grottos were a work of love and squirrel-like searching for stones, flowers, leaves, broken ornaments, texts and pictures from magazines. I once saw a little blue egg on a grotto yet the only birds I ever saw, all the time I lived in Poplar, were sparrows. Perhaps in my ignorance I thought all birds were sparrows. Winnie and Amy would place their grotto near a public house – clever Winnie, for they might catch a reeling man whose thriftiness was befuddled by an extra pint. Winnie was found out because a man gave her a lot of money for one kiss. This monstrous act was reported to Mother who promptly bankrupted the grotto business. After this, how could us younger ones start up in business? We felt the older ones had all the fun when they were young.

My best friend in Bath Street was Ivy White. She had an older brother called soppy Joe. He was quite elderly and always wore a blue serge suit and a bowler hat. He had a very big head with bloodshot eyes not placed quite straight in his head and he ambled about in a slow running way. Ivy told me her brother was silly because as a baby he had eaten a whole bar of carbolic soap by mistake. I thought this must be true because very daringly I licked a bar of carbolic soap at home. So terrible was this one light lick that I knew if a baby ate a whole bar it would send him silly. Why, it would even send a grown man silly, although of course a grown man was more sensible than a little baby.

My friendship with Ivy began to wane on the day of the

outing. I had no choice, for she had made me feel different from the other girls and spoilt everything. The poor children of Poplar were to be taken for a day's outing to the country by a welfare organisation. We were to obtain our tickets beforehand at a nearby vicarage. Ivy was horrified when I joined the queue for my ticket. 'Why, Dolly Chegwidden,' she said loudly, 'you can't come on the outing, you're rich.' This statement coming from my friend, a girl I thought the same as I was, shocked me and I ran home to Mother in tears, expecting her to deny Ivy's accusation. But worse was to come, for Mother looked pleased and said, 'To be poor and look poor is the devil outright.' I knew then I would not go on the outing with my friends. I wished Amy would come home, she would get my ticket. She had been on one outing for a day and another for a week, both for starving dockers' children. She just joined on the end of the queues and when the woman said Amy didn't look very starving, Amy still didn't run home in tears, she just acted her part out.

I went to see my friends off hoping that the woman at the brakes would see me and insist on my going, but Ivy was watching me carefully and I knew she would tell the woman I was rich, so I looked the other way when the woman smiled at me. I went home feeling I was happier when I didn't know I was rich. Mother said, 'Disappointments are good for young people,' which stemmed my tears because I felt angry.

One day the Sunday School included in an outing Len and Amy who left in the early morning with their sandwiches and a whole penny each to spend. The excursion was cancelled at the last minute but the vicar threw open the vicarage gardens for the children. Amy persuaded Len to spend his money while she was spending hers and finally they went home. 'Did you enjoy the day at the sea?' asked Mother innocently. 'Oh, yes,' cried Amy, 'it was lovely.' 'Then you are a little liar,' Mother said, 'for I have been watching you from the bedroom window.' Amy had forgotten that Mother could see across the railway to the vicarage gardens. Mother reproved her, and off Amy went to bed in a temper. First Amy paid a visit to Mother's room and tore the velvet off Mother's best hat, then satisfied she went to bed. Father grumbled at Amy for her sins, then she crept to his chest of drawers and tore into little squares some photographs Dad's best friend had taken of him. She did not put them down the lavatory through fright as I would have done. She laid them all out in his drawer so he could see them. Although I knew she was beyond the pale for the terrible revenges she took on those who crossed her, I thought she was as brave as any war heroine and I was secretly jealous of her. I could never have faced Mother's, 'Oh, Amy, Amy, how can you be so unkind?' I would have drowned in my tears, whereas Amy was pleased to the last. She would have made a wonderful suffragette.

6 A winkle-eyed lot

The Great War, or the 1914 war as we called it, the birth of my youngest sister, and starting school for the first time are all wrapped up in the same memories and I never knew which was the worst thing out of these three.

My father arrived at Valetta on the day that Marjorie was born and so she received the middle name of Valetta. I didn't know whether it was in honour of the War, the place or my father. I was very jealous that my young sister was famous because of her name, and I was annoyed that she had been born at all. When people would say, 'Little Marjorie Valetta, a war baby,' or Mother would say her last baby, little Marjorie, was a war baby, they all seemed to say it so proudly, and little Marjorie would look all modest. Yet I knew she felt pleased and famous, and I used to grit my teeth because I always wanted to say, 'Only just,' which would have earned me a sad glance from Mother.

I have hazy visions of my father going off 'to the front' for before leaving Mother in tears she had to help him lay all his kit out in the little back yard so it could be checked and inspected by him in a military fashion.

He didn't have to go to war, he was forty-nine and too old, but he had joined the Territorials to get a holiday each year and when war broke out, feeling guilty that he would have had a holiday without fighting, he volunteered for the Royal Fusiliers in London and gave his age as forty-six. Mother said he shouldn't go, but Father felt he must. He couldn't go back to the West Kents for they would have known his age, and he couldn't go with the Territorials for they knew it too. But I thought the Royal Fusiliers sounded lovely, like a bugle. He laid all the pipes in the trenches in France for the Pioneer Corps, and spent his fiftieth birthday at Ypres.

I thought, early on in the war, that the front was like a barrier at a railway station: the Huns would be waiting at this white barrier (it was always white in my imagination), and when my father arrived with his grey tool chest and his men, then battle would commence.

My brother Arthur, who was seventeen, followed my father to France very quickly, and as he was a gentleman in civvy street so he looked immaculate in his uniform. I was not concerned that two of the men in the family had gone, for lots of fathers and brothers were going to the front and I felt it had something to do with that terrible picture that was everywhere – on the railway wall, on the church railings, the bank, and ever so many on the police station walls. I knew it was a picture of Kitchener because my older brothers and sisters would play battles, but I hated the picture, for Kitchener had fierce yellow eyes which followed me all along the road. I used to walk backwards and in a circle and the eyes still looked straight at me. I touched the picture once and was surprised not to feel his pointing finger, for until I touched the poster I was sure his clenched hand and large stiff forefinger were sticking out from the hoarding and walls.

My father had a bearskin which had to be returned to his old regiment as he was now in a new regiment, but one day the older girls were playing battles and jumping up from the trenches caught the bearskin alight on the gas mantle. Someone was despatched to the shops for a new inverted gas mantle before darkness fell while Mother vainly tried to repair the bearskin. She tried everything, even horsehair from her mattress but the shiny black hairs on the bearskin now had mangy patches, and I remember it hanging on her bedroom door like a diseased cat or a cat that had been in a fight, for the cats in the Grove were always fighting and mangy.

My brother Charlie was only fifteen, and as soon as Father had left for the war he went out and joined up, although Mother cried and pleaded with him not to go. Mother always said her prayers and they were answered. Charlie was sent to the very district in France where my father's battalion were stationed. By another stroke of fate a Sergeant in my father's mess was in the Office when the new recruits were being checked in. He saw my father and said, 'Chick, there's a young boy with red curly hair who has just arrived from home. Christ, they're sending them out young now, this one doesn't look as if he's had his napkins off long; you wouldn't believe it, he's got the same name as you, Chegwidden.' Off my father went to the office but Charlie had been sent on and my father in a frantic state told the officer he thought the new recruit was his son, if so he was only just fifteen. The officer, a kindly man, traced Charlie who, much aggrieved, was sent back to his mum with some wounded. He bided his time impatiently and at the earliest age possible he joined the Royal Navy.

Only Mother cried when her men went, so it seemed strange that Amy should sob so when Arthur went off to France. It seemed impossible to pacify her, and all the more mysterious that she should act this way for she and Arthur were always at loggerheads. Her tears, alas, were not for Arthur but for what he took with him. Arthur always used to frighten us when we had anything new, for he was a tryer-on. It was an extremely rare event to own something precious of our very own and whatever was shown to him he just had to try it on after inspecting it minutely and we always clamoured for it back. Someone had given Amy a bracelet made out of elephant's hair. It was the first piece of jewellery she had ever owned and it meant the world to her. For one thing everyone knew that an elephant's hair bracelet was lucky and to us luck was everything. Arthur, dressed in his uniform and ready to leave, tried on this precious bangle and couldn't get it off. Finally he left for the front wearing the only thing Amy treasured. 'Never mind,' said Mother, thinking to stem Amy's tears, 'Perhaps your lucky bracelet will be the means of keeping him safe for us.' More tears from Amy, for the safety of the bracelet was her main concern and she was frantic when she thought that if Arthur were killed a little German girl might wear her bracelet. The period when Arthur was in hospital at Salonika must have been a worrying time for my sister.

Arthur became great friends with another young soldier and the two of them went all over France cutting wires so that the Germans would not know what our boys were doing. His friend was decorated, but Father said that as there were only so many decorations for so many battalions it didn't mean that Arthur was any less brave, and we all agreed. I knew that not even the decorated friend would cut his wires so beautifully and neatly as Arthur. He did everything so perfectly.

Not far from our house was a very nice baker's shop which people called the German bakers. They had been in Poplar for years and made the best bread in the district. Such a clean shop my mother thought and she cried when the shop was attacked by people during the war. It was said we should feel worried because of our name, which made me very angry, but was all right in the end because Dad and Arthur were Tommies and Charlie a Jack Tar.

The night of the Silvertown explosion remains vividly with me. One Friday evening Winnie and Amy were at Guides, Agnes had gone to live at Forest Hill at her fiancé's home as it was safer than Poplar, and Leonard was with David at the boys' club in the church institute. Mother was singing my favourite 'They played in a beautiful garden, those children of high degree' and she had just reached the saddest and loveliest part where the little crippled boy gazes through the wrought iron gates at the beautiful rich girl, when everything went scarlet. There was a terrific bang which went right through my ears, the windows broke and scattered glass all over us. Mother quickly dressed us and we went out into the Grove where it seemed everyone had gathered. Children were screaming and Mother thought the safest place for us that night, for we expected more explosions, was the crypt of All Saints. As we went round into the main road David was running towards us laughing and crying and he appeared to be quite demented. A 'Lady' lived in the corner house next to the estate agents which her husband owned, and she said she would give David some milk, which made me jealous, and put him to bed in her basement. Although it transpired that poor David had been blown across the hall of the institute and down the stairs by the explosion, I had no sympathy for him, for I knew 'boys don't cry' and I felt he was having rich treatment considering the fuss he was making.

When we reached the crypt it was full of old women, mothers and children. Behind us stacked in rows were a lot of wooden coffins and the old women kept cackling jokes about these coffins and I couldn't understand how they could laugh about anything so awful. Amy appeared wearing a sort of arm-band and carrying a jug of water. She had her ministering angel look on her face but she never came to us with water for we were only family.

There was a red pail which was put out for people to wee-wee in and I refused to do this. I was much too refined and modest a child, I knew, to do such a terrible thing in public. For one thing the noise the pail made when it was being filled was very loud so that even at Mother's coaxing that she would hide me with her skirts, I still refused. If people didn't see me I knew they would hear me.

The vicar came in carrying what looked like a large white enamel aeroplane, apparently it was part of an aerial torpedo which he said had just missed our lovely church and we all said a prayer of thanks because God had saved his house from destruction. We prayed for our brave boys at the front and then when news came that the night's explosion was at Woolwich Arsenal we prayed for the dead, dying and injured.

I hated the crypt with its coffins, its old women and its grey mouldy atmosphere. It had a real feeling of death and Mother said, 'Very well, then, we won't come again, we will stay in our own little house and God will look after us.' I think she was worried because I wouldn't wee-wee in the crypt. From then on, if the raids were still frightening, at least home was the best place to be if one is in danger or afraid. We would snuggle up on the pot board, tell stories and listen to Big Bertha the immense gun on Blackwall Point and the answering boom from her sister Annie across the river. Mother would have to get Winnie's supper ready before we took cover for she was always late, having gone to evening classes. She would have her supper underneath the kitchen table. It was dark but we knew when Winnie had reached the rice pudding stage for when she was the last one in hers was left in the large enamel pie-dish, and we could hear her scraping and scraping to try to eat all the lovely sweet sugary brown bits which got baked on the side of the dish. Amy hated this scraping noise but it made no difference to Winnie. Scrape she would as long as she wanted to. Not a fragment must be left.

The older girls spent a lot of their time queuing at the shops for food. The rumour would spread, 'They've got potatoes down Chrisp Street,' and they would be off like firemen sliding down poles. Hours later they would return like victors until Mother examined their buy and pronounced, 'Why, these are no bigger than peas. How am I to feed my hungry family?'

Food became a bigger problem later on for Father was reported missing, so his allowance was stopped by the War Office immediately. After all, if there was no father working or fighting, Mother couldn't expect wages. Mother was so worried about Father being missing that she got in touch with the Prince of Wales relief organisation. I don't know whether they gave food tickets, but they were very kind and traced Father for Mother. One of his men had taken Father's disc by mistake and was found killed in the trenches. I thought Mother cried at strange things.

One day an aunt sent her a whole 10s. postal order and Mother cried. Our country aunts began to send Mother trunks of old clothes, and night and day she would make clothes for all of us, sitting on the pot board, or on her bed. She made shirts for the little boys out of the tails of uncle's old ones, little trousers out of big ones, frocks, petticoats and pinafores, and her needle would flash in and out. She pinned the material to her knee and I was always worried she would sew through her knee as well.

Winifred was a tower of strength during the war because she was never afraid. A girl guide, she decided to get ready, to 'be prepared,' and she stressed this necessity to Amy who was in happy agreement. Winnie made what she called gunny bags, which were to hold all their treasured possessions. These bags would be tied round their waists at night after they had donned all the clothes they possessed. They had a difficult time climbing into bed each night so fully clothed were they, and much giggling and screaming went on before they finally achieved a horizontal position by rolling each other over. It was uncomfortable to sleep like that but if Winnie thought by being prepared she was doing the Germans one in the eye, that was all the encouragement she needed. Getting ready for work in the morning was a backward process. Winnie had been reading the *Hound of the Baskervilles* and one night she was reciting 'No moon, no stars, no Jupiter or Mars,' when the house shook with an almighty bang and two enormous girls fell down the stairs to the kitchen. It was the first night Big Bertha had fired a salvo.

On the day that the North Street infants' school was hit, Mother had given me some red gooseberries and I was standing at the top of the Grove enjoying a feast. I was biting into each gooseberry saying, 'Here's the church, here's the steeple . . .' when I noticed some aeroplanes overhead puffing little clouds of smoke. Then Big Bertha started firing. In spite of the bangs, I went on eating my lovely gooseberries and I was just thinking what a lot of hairs there were on them, when suddenly policemen came running along blowing whistles, stopping trams and carts and turning them all round again. I was just looking to see how many gooseberries I had left when across the road came a galloping coal-cart. The driver had on his back-to-front shovel hat and in the crook of one arm he was carrying a little boy who seemed asleep, but the little boy's face was covered with something scarlet and so was his shirt. Running behind the cart was a woman in a pinafore and behind her another little fair boy in a white shirt, but it was the fair boy's face that kept my gaze. He looked so frightened that I thought somebody must be after him. I went home to tell Mother and she cried and I wondered if she knew the frightened little boy. She said I must stay by the front gate in future and later I learned from some other children that seventeen children had been killed while I was eating my gooseberries and ever so many had been injured. Then I realised that the Germans did not stay at the front with my father. It was different at the top of the Grove when we saw the Zeppelin shot down in flames. Everybody danced and cheered.

At the beginning of the war Winnie was already working in the City and Amy started work during the war. I don't think they worked very hard because they used to meet during the day, making some excuse about taking messages. One day Amy was hanging about in Fenchurch Street for Winnie, when there was an air raid and a horse's head was blown off. Of course Amy became hysterical and some City men had taken her down a basement to shelter when a man rushed in and said a young girl had just been killed. Off went Amy again, 'It's my sister, it's my sister,' she cried. A gentleman decided to escort Amy to Winnie's office to impart the sad news and when this sympathetic gentleman and a sobbing Amy arrived, Winnie was sitting in the outer office of her firm enjoying a large sticky bun. She was indignant at the fuss and said Amy was a stupid idiot and should get back to work. Poor Amy.

We would go for walks near the docks on Sunday mornings and wonder where the children were whose houses were cut in half. Once we saw a little kitten mewing and my friend took it home.

The King and Queen came to Poplar during the war to cheer us up and visit the little children injured at North Street school. They gave presents to the wounded children – one boy of four received a large coarse shirt for a working man, which had no collar. My friend said it would not fit the little boy's father for he was only a tiny man. It didn't seem fair to me that the little boy was injured and his father got the present, and suppose his father was in France, he might be killed and not need a working shirt.

Some friends of ours took shelter in a High Street school

during the raids. They would all sleep in the hall of the school having been told it was the safest place in Poplar. Because the school was surrounded by streets of houses there was no room for a playground, and this had been built on top of the school and covered over by wire netting. The experts informed the shelterers that any bomb landing on Dingle Lane school would bounce off the wire netting, and I wondered if it would keep on bouncing until it reached the river.

By lucky chance Father and Arthur arrived home on leave from France on the same day and it was decided that a family portrait should be taken, not only as a monument to posterity, but as Mother sadly said, 'It might be the last time the whole family are together.'

An appointment was made at Whiffen's the photographers in East India Dock Road for twelve people could not just march in on the off-chance, and a Sunday morning was arranged for this great event. All the girls, and the younger boys, were very excited, the girls rehearsing beautiful poses and romantic smiles ready for the day. Dad and Arthur spent hours on their spit and polish routine while Charlie ignored the whole proceedings.

Mother rose early on the Sunday morning to prepare as much of the dinner as possible, and after breakfast we younger ones were dressed in our Sunday best and asked to sit quietly until the older ones were ready. Cecil kept dashing off at every opportunity and had to be hauled back. In the end Mother had to change the boys' white blouses for blue jerseys. My frock wouldn't show the dirt because it was navy blue. Miss Cook, a court dressmaker, who lived next door but one and was very fond of us, had made it for me, and thinking it would please me she had made a bright silk collar for the plain frock. I loved the silky feel of the collar which was striped with all colours of the rainbow.

There were so many arguments for Mother to settle, so much pouring of oil on troubled waters, she had less free time than anyone for her own preparations. Agnes was in tears. Although she had a new cream tussore frock with a lace collar she also had new shoes, and she thought her frock would be too long and so hide her shoes. When Mother said the oldest ones would be at the back of the photograph, therefore her shoes would not show in any case, her tears flowed so fast she was advised to go and bathe her face. Winnie had won a watch. It was a cheap gun-metal affair but the first watch in the family and she was anxious to show it. Future evidence of her past affluence. Mother suggested that she stood behind Cecil and rested her hand and wrist on his shoulder. In this way not only would the watch be shown but it would also capture sisterly love, especially if Winnie wore a tender expression. Amy had hogged the mirror, not only to try out different hair styles but also different film star expressions. Mother said vanity was a besetting sin which Amy resented, to say the least of it.

Finally when we had all been inspected and passed muster Charlie was missing and to the family's disgust he appeared with a silk muffler around his neck. Father ordered him to put on a collar and tie, and when he finally appeared he was wearing a soft collar with his tie. There was no more time for any further delay and we all climbed up the wooden stair-case to glorify and amaze the outside world (especially the neighbours). Father carried baby Marjorie, gave Mother his arm and the Sergeant and his Lady sailed down the Grove followed by the motley results of their union. Arthur, that immaculate soldier of the King, looked round at the rest of us, and, who shall blame him, decided he could not face public association with us and marched off alone, in a mili-tary manner, to Whiffen's. Agnes, still sniffing, took my hand, Winnie walked with her hand on Cecil's shoulder practising the watch position. Amy followed alone, checking that her two ribbon bows were still fluffed out, and David and Leonard didn't walk but seemed to fall about laughing at nothing.

As the photographer ushered us into his studio he gave Mother's hand a squeeze and whispered sympathetically that he was going to produce a wonderful photograph. I suppose he thought that, with two members in uniform and one more nearly of fighting age, it was a good-bye gesture. The studio was a dim musty-smelling room, something like a cavern. The walls appeared to be covered with a sort of shiny canvas on which had been painted rustic seats, urns of flowers, and in the centre, a large pink lady with fluffy dark hair, and a very low-necked flowering dress. She wore a rose for modesty at the bottom of her cleavage and, holding a fan, she was glancing up coyly at a young man in scarlet uniform. He had a sword at his side. As the canvas was somewhat cracked with age and bulged from the walls in places, at the entry of such a large number of people, some rushing, a displacement of air took place. The lovers' expressions changed so comically with the moving canvas that Len, who was really trying to control himself, let out a sort of high strangled squeak, which set half the family off into giggles.

At last the poor photographer got us all into position and more or less subdued but when he said, 'Watch the birdie,' Len said to Dave, 'Don't look up,' and the photographer flew out from under his large black cloth. But all was then still and silent. He said, 'Now, all smile please,' but Winnie's arm bearing the watch had somehow crept right down to Cecil's hips. From then on it became a silent battle between the photographer and Winnie, she trying to judge the exact moment he would take the photo, he knowing she was doing this and determined to get the better of this obstinate female. All this time Amy had been taking her dramatic poses so that because of the prolonged battle which had been taking place, she had lost the sense of timing she needed to hold the pose long enough. At least the photo was taken when she wasn't ready, so the photographer had beaten Winnie in the end.

When the photograph was delivered at the little house it caused amusement, anger, satisfaction and disappointment according to each one's opinion of their 'likeness.' Mother always took a good photograph. Dad looked like the father of Tallulah Bankhead. Arthur, left hand on hip, looked like a soldier for the Queen. Charlie was pleased his soft collar appeared as a muffler. Agnes and Amy, the two prettiest girls, came out the plainest, indeed Amy had moved and was on the cross-eyed side. It was obvious Len was trying to stop laughing and Cecil one could see had been giggling. David came out very sad-looking. The whole family agreed the photograph had been very kind to Dolly. At the time I was pleased with this unanimous compliment. Although Mother laughed every time she looked at it, she thought it was lovely and extravagantly ordered a framed enlargement which had a permanent place of honour on the front room wall at No. 13.

Father had the final word, apt as usual. He said we all looked a winkle-eyed lot.

7 Marjorie V.C.

We moved house during the war while Father, Arthur and Charlie were away. It came about in rather a strange way and I think it was because Mother had taught us all manners. Further down the Grove in one of the bigger houses lived a maiden lady, a Miss Walker. She would say, 'Good morning, Mrs Chegwidden, I hope you and your family are well and you are still receiving good tidings of your men at the front.' Then Mother would say, 'Good morning, Miss Walker. My family are all well, thank you, and I hear from my husband and the boys from time to time.' My mother always said, 'My husband'; my friends' mothers would call their husbands either 'Mr So and So' or 'my old man,' but Mother never referred to my father as Mr Chegwidden, always without fail, 'my husband.' Miss Walker was very fond of children and carried in her handbag a long round tin filled with peardrops, which she would offer to us children, and Mother told us not to rush up to Miss Walker because of the sweets. However, there was no danger we would miss a sweet by not tearing up through the little house to catch her as she passed, for she always hesitated and looked down at our area. She never gave us a sticky peardrop but always offered us the tin, and laughed at our struggles to take only one, often popping an extra one into our mouths.

She called on Mother one day to say she was moving to the country and if Mother would like her bigger house, no. 13, it would be 19s. per week and an agent would call every Monday for the rent. She added that she would very much like to feel that the dear children were living in her house, it would make her very happy. Mother was 'over the moon,' not only because she hated the little house but because Miss

Walker's offer was a compliment to her on the way she had tried to bring us up. Who else would have wanted such a crowd in a house they owned but dear Miss Walker?

I was glad to be away from that grown-up boy next door who held a sixpence in his hand, and whispered in a nasty hoarse voice when the girls who were not grown up went through the yard, 'I'll give you sixpence for a look.' All the girls ran frightened indoors. Sixpence was a fortune but we knew he was a nasty boy-man.

The day we moved I said goodbye to our little house. I went into the tiny yard and removed the loose brick from the wall. It was my secret place for my treasures, although all I ever had in it was my 'bonce and gobs' (five-stones); the bonce was a real ball but the gobs were just rounded stones I had collected, but with use they had become just right for bonce and gobs, and I was a champion.

I looked at the drain and wondered where the horrible eel was now. Mother came into the yard and must have read my thoughts for she laughed at my face and said, 'There is no worry now, he's probably swimming in the North Sea.' I thought of a huge black monster in the ocean and hoped he wouldn't turn over the ship that Charlie was a sailor in, but if the thing had turned the ship over I would still rather it was in the North Sea than anywhere near me. I remembered the day of its escape and I shuddered, but anyway it was Charlie's eel so he was to blame if it was causing trouble anywhere. He had brought it home as proudly as if he'd been on a dangerous mission and had captured it at the risk of his life. Because he was so pleased and excited about this creature Mother tried to hide her fear and dislike of the wet and slimy reptile.

Charlie said if it were taken care of it would grow as large as a boa-constrictor and it was tenderly placed in a pail of water in the tiny back yard. He fed it regularly and it really did begin to grow. To me it seemed enormous. I was terrified of it, it seemed to know when I was going through the back yard, for it swam round in its pail and looked straight at me with its two wicked eyes. When Mother was hanging out the

67

washing and looked at this snake up went her shoulder and in went a little siphon of breath. My brother used to stroke it and talk to it. Goodness knows what he intended to do with it, for it was getting too big for its pail. Would it come into the house looking for more water? I used to cling to Mother's skirts tightly on the way to bed, pleased when all the windows were closed, and this serpent was with me in my dreams. What it would do when it found me I never dared to think, and an invitation from my brother to touch it sent me into hysterics.

My day of salvation came in the shape of little Marjorie. Whether she was just being curious about the eel (she was known as Miss Inquisitive) or whether it was an accident during play I don't know, but the eel's pail was knocked over and out slid the eel. Our screams brought Mother to the yard but with one terrified look she ran back into the house, whereupon I began to cry. I thought she had left me to my oft dreamt-of fate. I couldn't run after her for I would have to pass the eel and the yard was so small. If I ran out of the gate it might start to chase me. I knew that its life's desire was to get me. If I had been brave enough to touch it when invited, it might not dislike me so much now.

Just as I felt the eel was mesmerising me and I couldn't move, Mother came running from the house. In her hands she held her best pair of fire-tongs, which had been a wedding present. They were about a yard long, shining silver with round ends about the size of a penny, but they were hinged at the top and only an expert could pick up a piece of coal with them, for the two hinges seemed to swivel round and move the wrong way as you grasped a piece of coal. They went sort of knock-kneed. I felt ashamed to have thought that Mother would have deserted me. She advanced very slowly and quietly on to the silent snake but just as she was ready to close the tongs it made a lightning movement and Mother just missed it. Calmer now, and a bit more desperate, and perhaps brave, for it hadn't attacked so far, though of course it was now nearer the drain, she really lunged at the eel and at one time actually held it for a few seconds in the tongs, but their length was defeating her. She was like someone trying to eat spaghetti for the first time with giant chopsticks, although I doubt if a spaghetti-eater would have uttered the warlike cries Mother was uttering; the eel, however, perhaps bruised by the tongs became very lively and made fast for the drain. I thought perhaps his brothers and sisters were calling him from the sewers.

Mother really did have another chance to retrieve him and be decorated for bravery by my brother, but suddenly she smiled at me, stood back and let the tongs fall and I felt like cheering when the eel finally disappeared down the drain. Mother went back into the house with a guilty look on her glad face for now she would have to face the eel's sorrowing owner and prepare her story. She would never say who knocked over the pail, but the echo of her karate-like cries lingered on in that little yard.

There was great excitement and activity the day we moved to no. 13. Father and now two of the boys were away at the front, and there was no money for removal expenses, but we all helped. Mother had a neighbour to whom she had been kind, Mrs Nicholson, who was in Mother's opinion as good as any man. She was a thin, pale woman, very sad and tired-looking. She took the frames and windows out of the bedroom when the mahogany chest of drawers got wedged on the stairs. Marjorie was only four years old but she also helped and was given the china chamber-pot, the one with the roses on, to carry to the new house. I wouldn't have carried it even though Mother laughed and said, 'It is clean,' but Marjorie carried it as proudly as if she were carrying the crown jewels and seemed pleased when everyone laughed at her careful progress down the Grove.

When Mrs Nicholson saw the basement at no. 13 with doors opening on to the outside world from both front and back of the house, she said in awed and excited tones, 'Isn't it wonderful, Mrs Cheg, you will be able to have all the doors open to let all the nasty odours out.' This caused great merriment amongst us all, Mother trying to still our laughter and not to giggle herself, for she wouldn't have caused any hurt to her kindly, strong helper.

No. 13 contained six fair-sized rooms on three floors: the ground floor, although semi-basement, was much brighter and lighter than at the little house, and the kitchen, or living-room, had french doors which led into the area with steps up to the front garden and gate. The scullery had the same doors and steep steps leading to the yard and lavatory, which we all called the W, like a ranch, but Father always called it the W.C. or water closet, and on the red-painted door he printed in his beautiful white printing the capital letters W.C. I never knew why he did this for we all knew what it was.

On the ground floor, although it was quite above ground level and had a dozen or so steps to it from the front garden path, was the front room, our parlour, and a back room, my parents' bedroom. On the second and last floor were two large rooms, bedrooms for the family.

The front room had a bay window and there Mother lovingly placed her aspidistra after tenderly wiping it with a milky cloth. She visited Killwicks at Stepney and bought a green plush sofa and two matching armchairs. They had mahogany curved arms and legs and beautiful cream roses on the seats of green plush. A carved mahogany occasional table, a rug by the marble fireplace and a mahogany over-mantel with many mirrors on it completed the furnishing of this luxury room. Father was very cross when he arrived home from the war; he thought Mother was turning into an extravagant woman, for she was to pay 2s. 6d. per week for this new furniture. But she said, 'Well, Agnes, Winnie and Amy are at work and you, Arthur and Charlie will be start-ing, now that the war is over, it will be nice for them to have somewhere they can bring their friends.'

Father was not at all pleased and he only visited this ele-gant room at Christmas time, for he thought he was an eco-nomical member of the family having made his own chair. It was a monstrosity. A barrel. He had sawn some of the front staves of the barrel away, made a seat and arms and padded and upholstered these arms in some velvet he had found. He painted the barrel a horrible brick colour with some paint he had by him, then because he had to have things to last for ever he had wired the barrel round with strong wire, but where he had twisted the ends and cut the wire with pliers it was most hazardous for stockings and legs and it was something we all had to be wary of. He was like a circus performer when he sat in this barrel, for he could swing round, reach to the table, or the mantelpiece or wherever he wanted without alighting from his carriage. No one else could do it, for the barrel would roll over fiercely if anyone else tried to turn while sitting in it. It was unbalanced by nature.

We never gave Dad the satisfaction of knowing how very comfortable this barrel was but it was sought after by all the family when he was away, although at the sound of his approach the barrel-sitter would get out very swiftly, not because Dad would have minded, but because we had all insulted it so much we couldn't let him know it was like a pullman car. From this seat he would shoot expertly into his spittoon, and as I sat near him, reading, I almost grew up with a twitch, for although he never missed I was always worried he might. But now that we had an elegant front room the days of his spittoon were numbered and very soon it was gone from his life. When he said he missed it, I would have liked to say that he always did, but that would have been a lie, for he was as good as any cowboy in a saloon at the pictures. Dong!

We settled down happily at the bigger house. If thirteen was an unlucky number to some, it never seemed so to the Cheggies. If my mother brain-washed us into thinking she was a lucky woman, we were lucky people, God had been good to us, she did it so subtly it was like that whiff of chloroform at the dentist's, very pleasant, putting the accent on the nice rather than the nasty. 'You all have your faculties,' said Mother. 'You must all be thankful for that.' I thought some of the family had more faculties than others, but agreed that we were all normal. Now I wonder if we were, for none of us walked down the Grove on the way home. Some of us looked like competitors in a walking race all disqualified at the tape, for the magnetic pull of home was too strong for any of us to walk there. From four o'clock onwards every day at regular intervals could be seen one member of the family running madly towards no. 13, and we would start to call, 'Mum,' as soon as we turned into the gate.

We leapt down the steps to the kitchen and Mother was always standing by the door in her black frock, lace collar pinned with her brooch which had an amber stone in the centre. The white cloth was on the table, the kettle singing on the fire, we were home. It was a happy place of roaring laughter, fierce argument, but never a fight, never a quarrel and never a sulk. Peace began again immediately after a difference of opinion. Nothing was ever held over like a dark cloud, the sun broke through immediately after a storm, which at no. 13 was only a shower. In all my life I never once heard Mother say, 'I'll tell your father,' which almost every other mother said, and she thought a sulky person a dreadful person. Only once was she not standing waiting to greet me with a smile when I returned home from school. She was still smiling then but sitting down in the wooden armchair. She had walked backwards down the kitchen steps after getting milk from the dairyman and had split her head open, necessitating a visit to hospital for stitches. The cloth was on the table but it was a terrible feeling for Mother to be sitting and not standing. I didn't like it at all.

She did something unheard of in the Grove. She planted grass seed in the little front garden, and Father made window-boxes so that Mother could plant her favourite petunias. The morning after Mother had planted the grass seed I woke up early. I had been excited the evening before; I was sure the grass would have grown and the Chegwiddens would have a lawn the very next day. I rushed downstairs, splashed my face at the scullery sink; 'Never leave the house dirty,' Mum always said, and I went out to see the magic carpet. It was still black earth – what had gone wrong? – and there in the middle of the little front garden was a large printed notice standing up on a piece of wood for all the world to see; 'Please keep off the grass.' Mother was very amused and soon all the Chegwiddens came out to inspect the notice, all giggling. We couldn't recognise the printing and never discovered the wag. But the grass did come up, thinly, and from a distance, if you held your head low coming home from school, Marjorie and I agreed it looked shadowy green. Someone once gave Mother a present of a delicious Cox's Orange Pippin, and she planted a pip from this in a little red pot. It grew, with her loving care until it was four inches tall, when 'someone' inquisitive, accidentally snapped it in two. Mother bound it up with sticky rag and it was planted in the garden of the new house Arthur and his bride were buying at Beckenham. It grew into a fertile tree always laden with fruit and it was called Mother's tree.

One Saturday morning I decided that Marjorie, who was now grown up, being four years old, should come along with me to Poplar Recreation Ground. As it was so early in the morning we would be the first ones there and thus be able to choose any swing we liked. Marjorie, all excited, ran with me to the park. I was right, no other children were there, and the old woman in charge of the children's playground was only just unlocking the little padlock to the swings when we arrived. She had very bad feet and little pieces of her shoes were cut to let her feet out. Hairs grew out of little hard shiny bumps on her chin and I used to think she was very fortunate these bumps and long black hairs were only on her chin. My father had told us of the man he knew who had a long black hair growing out of a bump on his nose, and who one day had a fit of sneezing and thrashed himself to death.

I chose a big girl's swing, the end one near the railings beyond which was a very large shed. We never played in the shed for it always had a funny smell even though it was open-fronted and looked out across the park. Marjorie being happily settled on a babies' swing, I dismissed her from my mind. No harm could come to her in the children's playground. The old lady was in charge, there was a gate and railings all round our swings. I was happy, alone among the empty big girls' swings. At any time I liked I could change my swing, I could even have a go on all of them and in my dream world of plenty I swung joyfully on that sunny Saturday morning.

Suddenly a soldier came into the children's playground. I knew grown-ups weren't allowed inside the gate and I was puzzling why the old woman had not sent him straight out of the enclosure, when he approached me and began to push my swing much too hard. I was frightened and looked at the old woman, but she just smiled and I felt very embarrassed and miserable. The soldier then pushed my swing crookedly, I caught one foot in the railings and the swing stopped drunkenly. He helped me off the swing and holding my hand hard, he said his little sister was across the other side of the park and couldn't do her frock up. Would I come and show her how to do it? I said, very bravely, for Mother had stressed we must be polite and respectful to grown-ups, 'No, my mother wants me to go home straight away.' But he held on so tightly to my hand I couldn't pull it away and I went with him across the park to where we *never* went, for Mother always said we must keep away from the grown-up's part of the shrubbery. We went past the bowling-green and then reached the shrubbery where the old men sat, but it was too early for the old men. The lady who had looked after the park in war time came along in her breeches with the leather patches inside her knees, and her white shirt; she waved at me and I tried to go to her, but the soldier wouldn't let go of my hand and I still couldn't see his little sister anywhere. Then he sat down and took me on his knee and I began to cry. Just then the sun went in and as he put his hands round my neck it got darker and I thought there would be thunder.

I opened my wet eyes which felt heavy, and running across the flower-beds towards us were Mother and little Marjorie. Mother was shouting, her face was red and wet and Marjorie looked very indignant. I thought Mother should not be running over flower-beds for that was worse than treading on grass. All the notices mentioned about not treading on the grass, there was no need to mention the flower-beds because no one would ever do such a wicked thing as that, I had never heard of anyone so daring. I tried to call to Mother to get off the flower-beds, else she would go to prison, but my voice would not come. My neck was hurting, I ached all over and I wanted to be sick. Then the soldier threw me to the ground, a stone cut my face which began to bleed and the blood ran into my mouth all warm and salty and I just didn't want to worry any more, not even about Mother, but just go to sleep. I was so tired.

The soldier too ran across the flower-beds and Mother still kept running, not to me, but after the soldier; she was screaming now and the lady in the breeches came and picked me up and said, 'There, there, it's all right now, try to walk.' Suddenly I was holding Mother's hand and Marjorie, the soldier and two policemen and crowds and crowds of kids were walking along East India Dock Road towards the police station. I wondered vaguely where all the children had come from and thought that if they had all been there before, I couldn't have chosen the swing I wanted. The policemen were holding the soldier's hands behind him and walking him in a funny way. I felt embarrassed at the public spectacle I had caused and wished the policemen would not walk the soldier in that dreadful way. He couldn't escape now.

When we arrived at the police station the crowds still wouldn't go away and the policemen got very angry with them. When we got inside the soldier was taken off somewhere and Mother, Marjorie and I sat on some very thin wooden seats and waited for the doctor to arrive. This was an awful thing; although I knew the answers to the doctor's questions my answers contained words which made me feel shy, and after my examination we went home. I felt so bad for I had made Mother run all the way from home on a Saturday after she had carried the heavy shopping bags from Chrisp Street. Why had I been such a coward instead of running away? Father and David were having their dinner. David looked at me as though I was a wicked girl. Father did not look at me at all.

My troubles were not over, for Mother, Marjorie and I had to go to court where there was a judge and I had to stand in a box and tell all about that Saturday morning in the recreation ground. Again, as I did with the nice doctor, I stumbled over the right words I knew everyone was waiting for me to say and I had to look at the soldier and say he was the one who 'pushed my swing,' but I couldn't say it for I didn't remember his face. However, Marjorie stood up and gave evidence in such a manner that the judge complimented her and said she should really be Marjorie V.C., which I thought was strange for she *was* Marjorie Valetta Chegwidden. The old woman came to court and said she thought the soldier was my brother and she was told in future to challenge all adults out of bounds.

I did not go to the recreation ground for a long, long time after that Saturday, and then when I went again I was surprised to see a white marble statue beyond the entrance drive. Up white steps on a white plinth was the most beautiful angel imaginable. She had her stone eyes half-closed and was protecting the little children whose names were chipped out of the side of the monument. I counted eighteen names on the square tablet, names of the children who had died when the German bomb hit North Street school. David said the statue wasn't marble but white stone which would go grey in time. Some time after that Mother was visited by the authorities and informed that Dorothy needed a holiday in the country. This holiday would be arranged by the Children's Fresh Air Fund, a country holiday organisation who set poor children up after a magical week in England's beautiful countryside, a week of luxury and heaven a child would never forget. I was very excited that I should be chosen for this gift, the only one of the Chegwiddens favoured by the gods. Mother seemed a bit apprehensive, but the authorities overcame her feeling of anxiety and the great day came for my transportation to heaven. I was taken by a stern-faced woman, with icy hands, to a railway station where I met more excited girls. We all had huge labels tied to our chests announcing we were from the East End and on our way to a Country Holiday Fund resort called Maidstone, in Kent.

We were sorted out at Maidstone and with two other girls I was delivered to a little terraced house in a street which looked just like the streets at home. Another stern woman read the Riot Act. She seemed to think because we were slum children we had come to destroy her home and she pointed to a cane hanging up on her kitchen wall. The other two girls and I slept in a single bed in a little box-room. They were tall girls and it was obvious from the start I should have to do as they told me. We had the same meal every day, mashed potato with little thin streaks of bright red cotton in it, and tiny bits of bone. I think the cotton was meat but I wasn't hungry and the woman said she supposed I wasn't used to good food. We were not allowed in the little front room and stayed in the small back garden all day. I counted the days until I could go home again.

The woman next door also had country holiday fund children and asked our benefactor, 'What are your lot like this week?' and they worked out how much money they had earned that summer. If they weren't pleased to have us, and that was obvious, they were very pleased with the money. The great day came for our departure from Maidstone and our woman said some children didn't know when they were well off for we had been given the chance of health and happiness in the country, and she seemed to think, because we were excited to be going home, that the East End children were an ungrateful lot. I was going home to where I was loved but such a woman wouldn't have understood that.

Mother had tears in her eyes when she saw me at the station and she sighed every time she looked at me. My father said, 'That's your country holiday fund for you. Dolly looks as though she wants a good disinfecting. They have to have so many on their books, you know.' He seemed in an awful temper, perhaps his pride was hurt because I had been the object of charity. Mother bathed me and she and I stayed up after the others were in bed for my head was itching and so I could not be with the others. She made a white paper collar for my neck and kept washing my hair in some smelly stuff again and again. Then I went to sleep with my head resting on her lovely bosom while she combed and combed every individual hair. She was very sad.

Next day Sister Kathleen came to see the healthy transformed Dorothy. She tutted and said, 'Better a dinner of herbs,' and she would arrange for me to have a sunbeam friend. Mother didn't want me to but Sister Kathleen insisted, and a few days later a letter came addressed to me: 'Miss Dorothy Chegwidden.' It was very exciting. It was from a rich lady in Wiltshire to tell me she was my sunbeam friend and I could choose two presents from the list she enclosed. I was so excited for the list began with a doll and doll's house and a doll's perambulator, and ended with a book and a tea-service for dolls. Mother just would not let me choose the first two presents on the list, thinking I was greedy, and in the end I was guided to ask for a tea-set and book. The little tea-set was very pretty with Japanese ladies on it and the book was a book on how to be a good needle-woman and make samplers of texts and run and fell a seam on chemises. Each page started off with a moral about naughty girls not receiving the rewards that good girls do.

The tea-set was so lovely I put it away in the bottom of the musty little cupboard in the kitchen, inspecting it occasionally like a miser inspecting his gold. One day I had a terrible shock. Someone had played with the tea-service and had broken a cup. Mother bought another cup but it didn't match the others and I never inspected it again. Mother didn't know or was not quite sure, who had dared to make tea in the lovely Japanese tea-set, so there was no one to accuse.

8 A mixed infant

Grove Villas was midway between two Schools, North Street, and Woolmore Street. My brothers went to North Street and we girls went to Woolmore Street.

Woolmore Street Mixed Infants School was a one-storey L-shaped building on one side of the road, and the big Girls' and Boys' School was a large two-storey building opposite, boys on the upper floor, girls on the ground floor. The playground was divided by a wall in which there was a green door, always locked, and woe betide any boy who climbed the wall to peep into the girls' playground. Our teachers were stern and strict but the boys' teachers were really harsh. I once saw a man teacher stamp on a boy's foot in temper. The boy was not wearing shoes or socks, and this was not an uncommon sight, even in winter. I loved the sound of the boys singing in the Hall above ours. 'Who is Sylvia?' and 'Clang, Clang, Clang on the Anvil,' for I always felt the boys sang more sweetly than the girls.

I started school eagerly enough for the tales of excitement and adventure my brothers and sisters told of school life were great, and Marjorie and I used to play schools at home. I was bitterly disappointed in the real thing. It couldn't be the same school my sisters loved.

I thought it silly to call my class the babies' class when most of us had younger brothers or sisters at home, and I knew I was grown-up. I was not a bit taken with the tiny chairs and tables. The chairs had curved arms and just enough space to get in properly. The teacher gave me a metal bowl and a small square of coloured bandage, and showed me how to shred it into cotton. This seemed silly to me. What could anyone do with little bits of cotton? When I was thinking how my back ached, the teacher took all our bowls away and gave us shallow tin trays covered with coarse gritty sand and we made letters in it, but the sand kept shifting about. I was one of the milk children because I was delicate, and in the morning I had to go to a cloakroom and drink a mug of milk. It had skin on top and was warm. I didn't like it much and then a lady in a green overall said she would give me a big spoon with lovely toffee in it, but it was fishy and tasted round my teeth all day.

Mother said perhaps it would be better in the afternoon, but when I went back after dinner it was worse, for we all had to put our heads down on the table and sleep. My head was on the table for years and years and the teacher looked as if she was sleeping. The little white knob on the blind was banging on the window in the breeze, and woke her up and when she climbed on to a chair to adjust the blinds, I could see her thick navy-blue bloomers. I wondered what Mother was doing and if I would ever go home again. Then a teacher went up and down the corridor ringing a noisy bell and Mother came to fetch me.

It was much better in the big girls' school. As I had hated the infants' school, well not hated, but it was yawn-making, though I was never frightened there, so I loved the big girls' school, even though I was frightened there at times. I never understood why I could be so happy where I was sometimes scared. My friends insisted they hated school and Dolly Chegwidden was crackers, but we all had fun, especially in the playground, so I felt they couldn't really have hated it. For one thing, they were not afraid of the cane or the black punishment book and thought I was a coward to be fearful of such things. But they, most of them, had knocks at home. I had never been slapped in the whole of my life, and I thought it must be the most painful thing in the world, even though the teachers always stated, when caning a girl, that the worst punishment was the entering of their names in the black book, for it would be there until eternity for all to see. 'Yah, it never hurt me' was the attitude of my comrades to punishment. To me they were as brave as soldiers.

I was never late for school, thanks partly to Mother and

partly to Polly. Polly was the grey and pink parrot one of my sailor brothers had brought home. Gradually it became as chattering a member of the family as any of us. It would scream, 'Cecil, Cecil, Cecil' every morning, then 'Late for school, late for school,' then 'Amy, Amy, Amy,' we just had to be on time. Marjorie would say, 'I'm not late for school, Polly, so you've got the time wrong.' Amy would glare at it every morning, and Mother would cover it with a cloth, for it didn't always seem to be able to count when we were all downstairs and would continue berating what it thought was an extra laggard.

The teachers were all strict, but many were sort of neutral, neither kind nor unkind, almost as if they didn't know we were there and would carry on teaching automatically even to an empty class. They were somewhere else at the time in their minds.

There was Miss Pepper. She looked like a standing-up baby hippopotamus, for her neck was so short her head seemed to join her shoulders. She had such a small snub nose that it was really only two nostril holes and her bosom was so huge and her legs so thin I could never make out at what part of her body the change took place and thought she must look like the drawings of people that tiny children did. She wore pincenez spectacles on a chain which dangled over her bosom like a mountaineer's rope over a precipice. We could always send Miss Pepper to sleep on a hot summer's afternoon when droning away at tables, indeed we got tables-saying to such a sing-song rhythm that we almost nodded off ourselves. We all knew our tables.

Miss Church was the teacher who played the piano and taught us to sing. Her pebble glasses were so thick that she seemed to have thousands of eyes in a tunnel and she was very good at netball. She wore brogue shoes and thick stockings on her thick legs. Miss Pepper wore black shoes with high heels which perched her bosom forward and made her take little running steps all through the hall, but Miss Church took strides like my sister, Winnie.

The head teacher, Mrs Russell, was the most frightening

person in the school. She was not quite the headmistress, for the real headmistress, a Scottish lady with long green silk frocks and black flat-heeled shoes, who walked with her hands behind her back up and down the school hall all day, finally disappeared. I thought she must have walked on to another school by mistake. To my sister and my contemporaries, the head teacher *was* the school, her name, Mrs Russell, for ever on our lips. Little Tillie, a thin half-starved looking girl, was for ever dropping off in class and Mrs Russell would advance on her, shake her like a dog shaking a rat and march her up and down to wake her. One day she caught Tillie's head on the corner of the desk and Tillie passed out and had to be carried out of the class. Mrs Russell never shook Tillie after that. She was thin with the usual large bosom and would put her face almost on top of a girl's and hiss remarks so that we were forced to gaze into the large open pores on her face. When the girls had needlework lessons she would bring her husband's clothes up to be mended. I could understand this because my mother, a wonderful needlewoman always hated mending men's clothes. One day Winnie, not afraid even of Mrs R., decided to try on Mr R.'s long winter pants in the teacher's absence. Unfortunately she put two of her fat legs into one leg of the pants and was trapped amongst noisy and hysterical girls when Mrs R. returned and meted out justice. Winnie still laughed all the way home.

Mrs R. caught Agnes swinging on the blackboard. One of the girls pushing her let go when Mrs R. appeared and Agnes catapulted on to the teacher's desk upsetting the ink. Agnes nearly lost her chance of higher education then, because such a thing might have affected the character Mrs R. gave her. Agnes had been too young for the scholarship one year and the next year the date was altered and she became too old, and she went on to a new type of school which had sprung up, a central school called Thomas Street, near Limehouse. Limehouse was my favourite place, near the lovely river and ships, tall houses down narrow causeways, a churchyard all grey and dreamlike with a pond in the grounds full of beautifully coloured goldfish. I could have lived at Limehouse for ever.

Everyone was frightened of Mrs R. but she seemed to treat the Chegwidden girls very leniently, always praising my elder sisters to me, and seemed only to pick on the thin, not so clever girls, which upset me. When Amy was Rosalind in *As You Like It*, Mrs R. made her costume and sewed lovely pearls all over the cap for her head. One day the headmistress was in class talking to Mrs R. when there was a terrific bang. Mrs R. said, 'There, headmistress, you see what I have to put up with, those boys have thrown stones against my window again.' I couldn't believe boys would be so daring, not at Mrs R.'s window. The headmistress said Mrs R. should go with her and look into the matter. Great joy from Mrs R., the light of battle shone in her eyes. Then my stupid friend Lizzie put up her hand. 'Yes,' said Mrs R. in a bad temper at Lizzie delaying the execution. 'Please Miss,' said Lizzie, 'it wasn't them boys throwing stones at the window, it was my bladder what burst.' Silly Lizzie. Retribution for playing with her bladder in class, retribution for making Mrs R. in the wrong about the boys. Bladders were, of course, balloons, and Lizzie had an uncle who was always buying these for her. It was her life's joy to see how far she could blow up one of her bladders before it burst.

Mrs R. left when Miss Wilkie became the new headmistress. Life, for me then it became the best it ever could be. Although only twelve I had been in the top class for some time and there was nothing else I could learn. I could read, write, and do the sums taught in that school, so I was chosen (an innovation of Miss Wilkie's) as her prefect. She pinned on my dress a shield-shaped leather badge in the middle of which was a large 'P' in black. I was to see to Miss Wilkie's needs, open the high windows with a screw-like key every morning, collect the registers and give out the stationery. All this going to my head, I volunteered to wash up the teachers' dinner plates. The caretaker's wife cooked the dinners for the teachers. My teacher, Miss White, cooked her own, always steamed fish on an enamel plate. Since I had only the little hand basin in the cloakroom, with cold water and no tools, when I came to this enamel plate with grey fish skin left on it I got very bad-tempered. After I had stopped the sink up twice with fat and bones, I was allowed to boil a kettle of water in the teachers' sitting-room, but I hated this, afraid I should drop scalding water on one of them or myself.

Miss Wilkie gave a party to the teachers to introduce herself to them and I was despatched to the shops for the best salmon, tinned fruit, cream and brown bread and butter. The girls' mouths all watered.

I adored Miss Wilkie. I think she had M.A. after her name. She inaugurated a school choir, insisting I should be in it when we entered into competition with other London schools. She realised I couldn't sing, 'Let's hope the judges will be struck deaf on the day,' my brothers said. 'For their sakes,' added my father, but she said my lovely smile would appeal to the judges, and so I was placed in the centre of the front row and I learned to mime. Of course, we won the shield for our rendering of 'Little seed, oh little brown brother', and went everywhere singing this.

We had school plays and I was always the villain. Once I had an enormous stye on my eye and Miss Wilkie gave me an eyeshade. During the performance the stye burst and my legs went down between the tables forming our stage. The audience cheered at the downfall of the villain, and kept booing me when I came on. Miss Wilkie said I was a real trouper to carry on and extricate myself without faltering in my words, but I limped home bruised and bleeding and wondered who really liked being famous.

Miss White was my teacher and I often felt she was jealous because I was the prefect, for she always seemed to get at me and make me feel I was nothing really. Perhaps I was getting too big for my boots. Not one of my friends liked Miss White, she was so sarcastic. She would call a girl to her desk and for ages go on shouting, 'You gem, you beauty, you star,' etc. She could make us squirm. My needlework was the worst she had ever seen and because the teachers were worried when the inspectors came round, I was not allowed to work on the tucked and gathered chemises we were making out of unbleached calico. Mine was always filthy, according to Miss White, and I pricked my fingers so much there were always bloodstains in the gathers. I was then put in charge of cutting the cotton. The cotton was wound round the short side of a book and cut so that the pieces were very short. As fast as I had 'threadled' one piece, I would require another piece. One day Miss White was called away and to gain popularity with the class I wound the cotton round the long side of the book and the girls were delighted with the longer threads. When Miss White arrived back she was so angry at what I had done, I was not allowed to cut the cotton any more and she set me sums to do instead. I detested arithmetic and chewed my pencil down to the lead. I ate the wood to save the mess.

We sat for the scholarship before Miss W. became head-mistress and for this purpose were required to bring our birth certificates to school. About half a dozen of us kept for-getting these and Miss W. announced that any girl, forget-ting her birth certificate that dinner-time and saying, 'Please, Miss, I forgot it,' would be caned. I had escaped this punish-ment so far, and determined to carry on unmarked, I put the 'sustifikit' in the pocket of my dress at dinner-time. Miss Cook, our dressmaker, came in with a new dress she had made out of an old one of Winnie's. It was so lovely Mother said I could wear it to school, and so I arrived back at school covered in glory and it was not until the bell went that I remembered the certificate in my other pocket. I wanted to die and racked my brains to try to avoid the word 'forgot' which would bring down the cane on my hand. I dallied about so that I was last in the line of criminals.

There were five of us waiting for execution. Four times Miss W. asked each girl the question, and four times down came the cane. 'Well, Chegwidden,' said Miss W., 'and I suppose you are going to tell me you forgot too.' 'No, Miss White,' I said brightly, 'I failed to remember.' 'You gem, you star, you beauty,' said Miss W., but she didn't cane me,

85

and nobody thought it was unfair for we always took Miss W. literally. Perhaps she realised this fact, or perhaps Miss Cook's frock dazzled her. It was navy blue serge and across the yoke Miss Cook had embroidered it with narrow green and gold braid in a long squiggle. Miss W. sent me all round the school to show it to the other teachers.

She had never forgiven me for not 'winning' the scholarship, for the Monday the results were announced she said, 'Oh, and what happened to you, Chegwidden? Were you dreaming instead of concentrating?'

My sister, Winnie, had won the scholarship and gone to George Green's School amongst the paid scholars and received a grant for her uniform. Her name was in the school hall at Woolmore Street in gold letters on a shiny black board, and Miss W. seemed to think I had let Winnie and the school down in some way, but I knew why I had failed, because of my cowardice.

The scholarship was held on a Saturday morning at another school across the main road from the docks. Only the girls who had passed the prelim. were allowed to sit, and we all met on a freezing cold day in the strange playground of the enormous school. Mother said I must not worry about it for my fear would make me ill, I already felt sick, and she packed me some rich tea biscuits in sandwiches. I could think of nothing else but these buttered biscuits, longing for playtime so I could eat them, for the scholarship took all morning.

As the bell went for us to start, the girl in front fainted and was carried out. I was so engrossed in this, a teacher came up and ordered me to get on with my sums. The first sum told me I should not win the scholarship, for it was about men digging a trench in a certain time and I had to find out how many men and a half could dig it in another number of days. I'd never heard of half a man in my life. I felt in my pockets, yes, my biscuits were still intact. I didn't want to get them broken, anyway it was composition after playtime, I would write one that was marvellous. After playtime when the bell went the girl behind me was sick and the school caretaker came in with a bucket of sand. I looked at the list of subjects for the composition. Oh, lovely, there was one, 'Describe your favourite park or public building.' That was easy. I had done a whole paragraph before I realised I was describing the Poplar Recreation Ground. I couldn't do that, I might mention the nasty soldier, and I tried to turn the essay into a description of Tunnel Gardens. Then I knew I was describing too many parks instead of my favourite, and suddenly I thought, well what did a scholarship matter and I became quite happy having reached that decision. But I could have told Miss W. the result before she told me.

I was captain of the netball team. 'No one,' said Miss W., 'can get on to the ball so quickly as Chegwidden. It is really amazing.' We played other schools and I shone in Miss W.'s eyes. At netball only, I fear, for once in the absence of other teachers she took the whole school and when my hand shot up eagerly to answer a question she said, 'All right, Chegwidden, we all know that you know,' laughter from the girls, 'except at the time of the scholarship.' More laughter. I never answered a question of hers again.

Miss Wilkie decided to enter some of our compositions for an all London County Council contest and gave us the whole week-end to find a subject. After a sleepless week-end I was no nearer to a solution. I couldn't think of anything to write about. We had experienced the worst thunderstorm in living memory on Sunday night and tired and dejected I left for school. Passing the church grounds I was shocked at the sight that met my eyes. The enormous oak tree which stood in the grounds was the home for thousands of sparrows; the tree almost moved, mighty though it was, with the noise of their singing at evening time. We all loved the tree. This morning it was sad and wet-looking, for the ground beneath it was covered with hundreds of dead birds, all with caul-like eyes. They had been drowned.

I was feeling more miserable than ever when behind me in the distance I heard a jolly sort of music, and turning, I saw some elephants approaching! Leading them was a young man on a pony. He was carrying a placard advertising a forthcoming circus. The music cheered me up and the sight of the lovely elephants was an unusual treat. Across the road, Mr Samuels was just finishing polishing his fruits. He kept a stall outside his shop and the fruit, which he arranged on green grass cloth, was always red and shiny. Mr Samuels was a very well dressed Jewish gentleman with shiny shoes and a gold chain across his waistcoat. Everything about him shone. He was looking surprised at the music and the elephants, when suddenly the elephants wheeled left instead of going on down the road. They began to break into a sort of run towards Mr Samuels' stall; Mr Samuels dived under the green grass curtain of the stall into his shop and slammed the door just as the elephants reached his stall, where they demolished the fruit in no time at all and just ignored Mr Samuels' screaming and banging on the window. My brothers went to school in the opposite direction but they had come along to watch the parade and one of them was holding on to the station wall as though his legs wouldn't hold him up, laughing helplessly.

I now had a lot to write about and I thought about my father's elephants. When my parents were first married they lived near the Crystal Palace and one night my father returned somewhat merry from a regimental dinner. The road was dark and he slipped on something obnoxious on his front path. He managed to reach the steps to his basement door but when he went to go down them he found himself floundering about on something warm and rubber-like. Suddenly there was an unearthly scream. The windows flew open and Mother and the neighbours appeared with lamps. An elephant had escaped from a circus and wandering about in the dark it had got wedged in Father's area. The next day this poor creature was paraded round the streets in chains and my father said every now and then the other elephants would beat the escapee with chains. I cried when he told me that.

When the results of the composition contest were announced, Chegwidden of Woolmore Street, Poplar, had come top. I received a certificate and was over the moon, but no one at home seemed surprised or enthusiastic, and my friends at school couldn't have cared less. They were always talking about the day they would leave school, 'and get some money for our mum,' but my mother had never asked me for money. I never wanted any for myself although I nearly got pocket money after the war. Father lined David, Cecil, Marjorie and me up and said he would give us two-pence every Saturday. When he came to my turn he had run out of coppers and told me to 'ask your mother.' How could I ask Mother when I knew she 'had to manage,' but he didn't keep it up with the others either. Mother bought me the girls' paper each week and one week Cecil came in and snatched it from me. I should have waited for it back, but I was in the middle of a story about a boarding-school, and, snatching it back, it tore just as Mother came into the room. 'I will buy no more girls' papers if that is what is going to happen,' she said. Cecil laughed, but Mother was true to her word.

Fired with my composition success I entered the poetry contest. I wrote forty-eight verses about a cow and a donkey escaping from a cruel farmer. I was sure no one had ever written such a beautiful poem. When the results were announced I didn't even gain a mention and Miss White said perhaps now I would realise that what counted in this world was not quantity but quality. Nobody had told Mother that! Miss Wilkie sent for me. She had shown my composition to her friend, the headmaster of Millwall Central School and even though I hadn't passed the scholarship he would be pleased to give me the opportunity I deserved and accept me at his school. I was so excited I fell over twice on the way home and arrived with my knees bleeding and stockings torn which made Mother tut. While she was bathing my knees I stammered out my marvellous news. Mother said quite calmly, 'Thank Miss Wilkie for her kindness, but we don't think a mixed school is suitable for you.' My father had seen the boys and girls 'larking' about on the way home and had conveyed his views to Mother. There was no point in telling Mother I wouldn't lark about, I only wanted to learn to be a teacher. I told Miss Wilkie and she said, 'Such a pity, such a pity.' Still, Mother couldn't take my P badge away from me, and I knew she wouldn't want to. Why couldn't I have what the others had, why was Dolly different?

I was now old enough for the Girl Guides. I had listened avidly to the adventures of the other girls. Amy had badges from her wrist to the shoulder, Winnie was a lieutenant. They had such good times.

One day a princess was coming to inspect the guides in the local park. Winnie was the only one of the family to possess a Sunday hat. Mother received a grant for Winnie's school uniform and instead of buying at the prescribed shop, Miss Cook had made the school uniform more cheaply. Yet Winnie was thrilled and Miss Cook proud. The teachers all asked where Winnie obtained her uniform, and the paid scholars were jealous for Winnie's was tailor-made with better material. Mother had some money over from the grant. It was Winnie's money, said Mother, *she* had won the scholarship and she bought Winnie a cream straw hat with shiny cherries on it. No one had ever seen such a creation. Winnie kept it wrapped in tissue-paper and Amy envied and desired this hat more than anything.

On the morning of the guides' inspection Amy requested a loan of the hat. She wanted to impress her friends and perhaps the princess might see her. No, said Winnie, and off she went in her lieutenant's uniform. The princess had started down the rows of guides, standing to military attention when, across the park Winnie espied the hat. Amy was wearing it surrounded by admiring friends. Winnie shot out from the line of guides, and leaping all fences and railings in between she reached Amy, snatched the hat, thumped her and leaving her crying, re-leapt the railings and arrived back on parade holding her beautiful hat behind her back. She took it home, inspected it and wrapped it lovingly back in tissue-paper. But sadly one day she went to look at it and 'someone' had bitten all the cherries until they turned into cotton wool. The lovely hat was ruined.

Amy was a patrol-leader and kept her pack under tight control. Once at camp she roused them at dawn and ordered them down to the river to bathe. They were all tired as they'd had hardly any sleep, and they had been up late singing camp-fire songs. They reached the river and Amy ordered them in, but just as they got into the water, wearing only their knickers, a herd of cows came galloping down to drink. Forgetting her pack Amy was the first to scramble through the nettles and brambles back to camp, where they all queued at the first-aid station.

When her pack was on kitchen duty, Amy insisted on doing the cooking, urging them on to refuel the fire. Suddenly the flames got too high and her uniform was burnt from neck to hem. I met the guides on their homecoming from camp. They must have been in a storm for their round felt hats were misshapen and pointed, their clothes were untidy bundles of rags underneath their arms, and one or two had met with accidents to the elastic of their bloomers. They looked dirty, tired and unrecognisable from the military pack that had moved off so freshly a week before. The following year they went to the seaside at Littlehampton, and Mother had a telegram to say that Amy had met with an accident. Letter would be following, nothing serious. Apparently, some bright spark had suggested a donkey derby. Amy was a jockey, but either she had got panicky when her saddle slipped or the donkey went too fast. Not only had she come off but the donkey had fallen upside down on top of her. Dad said he expected the donkey was more frightened than Amy.

Mother said the guides wouldn't be suitable for me and I felt very sad when my younger sister, Marjorie, was allowed to join. I often wondered it if was the soldier's fault. Mother did worry about me. I wished I had been brave that day, perhaps I would have been a teacher, or at least a guide.

9 Nature's remedy

Mother spared no expense where a doctor was concerned for her children, although until now it had been a rare occurrence to have to call the doctor, the Cheggies were so healthy. At first we had Dr. Skelly, a grey-suited and grey-bearded man. He lived in a grey house in the main road and his surgery was in the basement. Always basements in Poplar. He invariably gave me the same medicine, cherry wine, pronounced delicious by the 'tasters' in the family, but of course it was the vilest concoction ever. Mother had implicit faith in doctors for me, but if she ever needed one for herself she never believed the doctor. The different young partners who came to Mother would say laughingly, 'Well, Mrs C., do you know what is wrong with you yet?' and Mother would say, 'No, but it certainly isn't what you said.' She would meet a doctor's eye as he entered her bedroom and say, 'Doctor, that medicine you gave me is of no use whatever, it has made me feel a lot worse.'

When she first had to wear spectacles the optician was trying her with a frame only, to get the correct fit, when Mother said indignantly, 'Well, these are no use at all. I really think I can see better without spectacles!' My father bought his spectacles on stalls in the market, second-hand ones, for a few coppers. Metal-framed ones which he hammered, soldered and padded until they fitted him, the lenses being the most unimportant part, it seemed. He was a do-it-yourself medical man, too, for he visited the little shop near Upper North Street, a dark shadowy little shop with a tiny bow-fronted window, Baldwins, and here herbal medicines were sold. 'You can't beat nature's remedy,' Father would say as he swallowed his rhubarb pills. This shop also sold female pills and it puzzled me why male pills were not sold there too.

Mother always said we were a lucky family and never made a fuss when she was not well, so we were shocked when she was admitted to Poplar hospital with suspected gall-stones. I didn't know how we could manage without her and it was a lonely feeling even though I had my brothers and sisters. Amy had two weeks' holiday and gallantly offered to be mother for that time, and promised everything would run on oiled wheels. She sincerely meant this and we had great confidence in her, although I knew I would not receive any special treatment regarding food I didn't like. It would be 'take it or leave it.' She fetched the battered alarm clock from Mother's room and we all went to bed transferring all responsibilities and worries on to Amy's willing shoulders. She was shining with maternal ardour.

The next morning, however, I realised we were living in a fool's paradise to think anyone could take Mother's place, for we were rudely awakened by Father's shouting, 'Bloody wars, gel, you'll have to do better than this, I'll get the sack.' We had all overslept. We rushed about leaving the house at minute intervals, without breakfast, tearing down the Grove as though our lives depended on it. Amy was very upset for she felt she let us all down. She could hardly avoid feeling this with recriminations pouring on to her shoulders from all directions. After all, she had possessed the alarm clock. She made up her mind to greet us that evening with a house spick and span and a truly delicious meal. Again we all believed her, for she really did mean it, but Marjorie and I arrived home from school to find Amy fast asleep. She had worked so hard all day attempting too much at once, washing, ironing, housework, cooking and, going upstairs in the late afternoon, had only sat on her bed for a moment. Exhausted she had fallen into a deep sleep.

Arthur complained that the collars of his shirt were creased and by Wednesday Amy had used up all the housekeeping which was supposed to last until Saturday. She had done lots of fancy cooking (with little cakes in crinkly paper to impress her boy-friend), and daily we were becoming more despondent, and, of course, bankrupt.

It wasn't any better for Mother. The hospital had decided to give her a starvation cure and on the Thursday when the doctor said she could have food again, she was given a piece of boiled fish which she said was as big as a walnut. The hospital sister then cheerfully told the doctor Mother had eaten a beautiful meal of lovely fish. Mother was feeling in a deprived mood therefore when Arthur and Father arrived for the visiting hour with their tales of woe and bankruptcy, not to mention rich food. Whether it was the minuscule size of the hospital fish or Father's low spirits, or whether Mother felt better, no one ever knew, but, much to the doctor's annoyance, she discharged herself, came home with Father and, without one moment's convalescence, became Mother again.

How different it had been for Father when he had been ill some years before at the little house. He did not disappear quietly and unobtrusively from our lives as Mother did, for we were woken one morning by the sound of a giant breathing painfully. The doctor arrived, diagnosed pneumonia, and ran from the house. Two policemen arrived with the wooden-slatted stretcher on wheels, the same stretcher which was used on Saturday nights to run a drunken man to the police station. But to show that Father was an accident and not a drunken man, the stretcher had an arch of black oilskin. Father was placed on the invalid carriage, wrapped in a red blanket, and strapped down. One policeman wheeled the stretcher while another walked by the side to assist its smooth passage along the bumpy road. Mother walked on the other side of the stretcher for Father was so ill she was going to stay with him through the crisis. The rest of the family followed the invalid down the Grove, those who weren't crying were trying to squeeze out a few tears for the sake of appearances, at the same time feeling a little ashamed that Father might be mistaken for a criminal because of the policemen and the wheeled contraption.

Mother came home so happy that Father had come through the crisis and one Sunday morning when she knew he was to sit on the balcony at Poplar hospital, she dressed us in our Sunday best and we walked to Poplar hospital to see him. We waited against the wall of the East India Docks until nurse brought Father out to a long chair. We crossed the road to the hospital railings. The older ones could see over the spearlike tops of the sooty iron railing, and the smaller fry squashed their faces in between the slats lower down. The nurse raised her hands when she saw us all, whether in surprise or horror I don't know, but she disappeared inside the french doors of the balcony and emerged quickly with two more nurses, one wearing a frilly baby's bonnet with a large white bow under her chin. They stared at us and we stared back, very respectfully of course, and when one nurse bent down and said something to Father we heard him shout in a strange voice which had gone all high and piping, 'Yes, and they're ALL mine.' He threw his arms wide and appeared very excited. When we came home and told Mother about Father's high voice, she said, 'Well, it was touch and go.'

So Mother was right to say we were lucky for her stay in hospital was brief, Father's successful, and Marjorie's visit very brief, but tragic for me, well, for my reputation. She was always fiddling about in drawers, or enquiring into things which had no earthly bearing on her circumstances, present or future, and even though I was reading an exciting book I was conscious of her ferreting. One afternoon Mother and I were in the kitchen and Marjorie was 'busy' in the scullery, when she suddenly called to me in a voice of excited discovery. I went irritably into the scullery where she was standing at the kitchen sink with father's cut-throat razor in her hand. She was holding it, open and aloft, and as I entered she said, 'This is marvellous. Look, it can even cut a hair off the back of my hand.' Before I had time to tell her to put such a dangerous thing away, she shouldn't have been going to Dad's cupboard in any case, with a theatrical sweep she drew the razor across her hand. The blade fell, slicing the back of her hand. For one horrible moment we both stood still, then she said, 'Oh, just look Dolly, you can see my bones,' and then the blood came pumping out. I yelled for Mother who grabbed the pepper pot, smothered Marjorie's hand and said, quite casually I thought, that Marjorie must go to the hospital to have it stitched. Mother said to Marjorie, 'Don't be frightened, you will have your big sister with you.' The big sister was apparently me. The first time I had been honoured with this title. Mother must have thought that in bestowing this title upon me at this time of crisis I would rise to the occasion.

Although feeling cold and sick I determined to succour my little sister even though I felt angry with her for her dangerous and unnecessary experiment. It wasn't so bad when Mother gave me 2d. for the bus fares to the hospital, I put my arm protectively round Marjorie and led her up the area steps. She *would* chatter on about the bones, the blood, the razor and I couldn't ask her to stop for I knew all ladies loved to talk about symptoms of illness and details of operations, but on the bus the blood began seeping through the towel, and the sight of this combined with Marjorie's vivid details, made me feel very far away and strange.

We got off the bus at Blackwall tunnel and as I took Marjorie's arm for support to walk the few yards to the hospital gates, the bus conductor, who must have been upstairs during our journey, leant from the bus and shouted rudely that we hadn't paid our fares. The bus was starting to move and I ran towards it with my 2d. The conductor insisted I wait for the tickets (he was honest if I was not, was the implication), and when I turned round Marjorie was disappearing inside the hospital. Now I felt so ghastly that the effort of opening the door to the casualty department caused me to stagger, for my knees seemed to be bending against my will. A fair, angelic-looking doctor approached me. 'Hold on,' he said, so kindly. 'You shall lie down, what is the trouble?' 'It's not me,' I stammered. 'It's my little sister, she's cut her hand on my Dad's razor.' He dropped me as though I were a leper, and I wondered why I had thought him angelic-looking, for he became very angry. 'Get outside,' he said, 'and put your head between your legs.'

The shock in his change of attitude shamed me so greatly that I found strength to leave the hospital, and when Marjorie came out looking like a cat that has got at the cream, I was sitting on the ground with my head against the wall, dying, I was sure. She helped me up and helped me home, still going into detail, this time about how wonderfully the wound had been stitched. 'It's exactly the same as needlework, Dolly,' she enthused. The thought of a needle going through flesh was the final straw and as Mother came down the Grove to meet us, I fainted.

Still no sympathy from Mother as I sat by the fire and sipped the hot sweet tea she had made for me. 'Well, you wouldn't be of much help in a crisis, I'm afraid, Dolly.' I glared at Marjorie who had given me such a wretched time, she was being treated like a heroine, and I had the rest of the family to face yet. My cowardice under fire would surely be repeated to each member of the family as they arrived home. Marjorie never reproached me, but her hand remained scarred and so did my reputation.

10 **Paper tiger**

Six days shalt thou labour, says the good book, but for my mother Sunday was not the day of rest scheduled by the scribes. On this holy day we were all at home getting under her feet. Mother rose just as early on Sunday mornings as she had done every day of her life, often leaving a sleeping household to go to Holy Communion at All Saints, and she had done some hours of housework before the family came straggling down in ones and twos. If no one was coming to tea she was able to have a few hours rest on Sunday afternoons, for then the house would be quiet with Father dozing in his chair, spectacles on top of his head and his library book swaying drunkenly in his hand. The younger ones were at Sunday school, the older ones visiting friends or taking a walk.

I remember one Sunday morning vividly for it was my first experience of physical violence in our house. My brothers had become interested in boxing and intended to join a boxing club. My father was very pleased he had sired men boys but Mother was most disapproving, for she thought boxing a coarse and cruel sport, and could not understand how one man would wish to hurt another. She was disappointed that any of her boys should wish to take up what she felt should not be called a sport. Father dismissed Mother's disapproval as a weak and feminine attitude, and made matters worse by actually obtaining two pairs of boxing-gloves and promoting himself to tutor, so that the boys would be in a position to protect themselves when they joined the club. No novices they, under Father's instruction.

The small back yard was to be the boxing-ring and to this spot we all repaired much to Father's annoyance. He insisted it wasn't a suitable spectacle for the feminine sex, but this made the girls all the more eager to stay. Perhaps he was embarrassed by the critical audience he knew he would have while teaching his sons the art of fisticuffs. His exasperation reached breaking-point when the ginger man next door, the pigeon-fancier, stationed himself on the garden wall and gazed silently, but somehow gleefully, at the instructor. Since my father had nothing in common with the neighbours, only ever giving them a polite but cursory nod, the interest of this man was the final straw, so back we all came, pouring through the scullery past Mother's cold looks, into the kitchen.

The small space between the dresser and the kitchen table would do for a practice ring and Mother was warned not to keep coming in and out for the door would open right into the middle of the ring, either separating the two opponents or subjecting her to an unintended blow. My father gave a practical demonstration of what boxing was all about, much to the impatience of the boys, who just wanted to be left alone to slog it out. He assumed the elbows upward Corinthian stance of the bare-fisted pugilists of the past. He always had a strange way of explaining things for he talked in actions more than words. My mother seemed to understand his waving hands, nodding head, and shrugging shoulders always, not to mention the movement of his eyes, and seemed for ever interested. I never could and gave up trying. Marjorie seemed fascinated by Father's sign language, although she couldn't understand it, and I knew she never would. She sat with a permanent stare when Father was drawing his day's doings to an interested Mother.

He was like a ballet-dancer prancing about the 'ring' and it was all very entertaining, but eventually the lessons were finished, the boys away to other pursuits. Father, satisfied he had done his paternal duty, went back to his book, a little doubtful that his sons had been intelligent enough to grasp his 'simple' tuition. Winifred, the strong athletic member of the family had been fired with enthusiasm by the lesson and putting on a pair of boxing-gloves, she challenged all and sundry. We were all too sensible to accept the challenge, but

Father, in a weak moment, said he would have a little spar with Win.

He sat in a chair while his gloves were being tied for him, giving Win last minute hints, and as he got up from his chair, still instructing, before the silent bell had gone, before he was ready and while he was partly off-balance, Winifred caught him with a right upper cut to his jaw, putting all her strength behind it. Father seemed to go up before he went down, knocking his head on the dresser. His elbow caught on the dish of hot prunes Mother had placed there to cool and as he slithered to the floor the hot brown sticky juice ran down his bald head. He gazed at Winnie like a goose looking down a bottle, bravely attempting to get up, until he saw that Winnie, having tasted first blood, still had the light of battle in her eyes and was waiting on prancing feet to deliver the final knock-out blow. Winnie commenced the victory count as Mother came in at the noise. She looked crossly down at Father and said, 'I would have thought you could have found something better to do, Walter, than indulge in horse-play with the girls.' She was annoyed at the waste of the prunes and the sticky mess everywhere and this brought Winnie to her senses, and peaceful again she began to help clear it up. She was smiling broadly as my father approached her and said, more in sorrow than in anger, 'You shouldn't have done that to me, gel, always remember, play fair, play fair.'

Fate still had another shock in store for Father that Sunday. He was to bite the dust again, this time because of my stupidity and absent-mindedness. We all had our regular places at the table. I always sat next to my father, and that dinner-time I was the last to reach the table, my mind still in the Doone valley with Jan Ridd. My father had risen from his chair to reach across the table, and not realising we were a chair short, I took my father's chair and sat down. Suddenly he came backwards into space. As he fell he grabbed the tablecloth and his hot meal showered on to him. The floorboard cracked and I thought he had broken his back. My mother came in from the scullery, still cross with my father and said irritably, 'Whatever are you up to now, Walter?' which made David say, 'You mean, down, Mum,' sending him off into roars of laughter at his own joke which he thought extremely clever and quick-witted. As my father rose, holding his back, he turned aggressively to me and said, 'Practical jokes are not only bloody silly things but they can cause permanent damage. Don't you ever play a practical joke on any one again.' Since I hadn't been joking and wouldn't dare to do such a thing and because I was relieved that my father had risen from the floor for I had been certain his back was broken, I burst into tears. This upset Mother who said to Father, 'Now Dolly won't eat any dinner,' thereby again putting the blame on the poor innocent man. 'I think I'm a bloody sight safer at work than home,' he shouted. Winnie fetched him a chair, still beaming and wearing her invisible laurel wreath, the boys were still laughing and Amy was looking secretly pleased. I had a headache.

My mother had a fund of pronouncements which she delivered from time to time with such a severe and serious mien, I felt these sayings were invented for me, and I believed all her trite remarks implicitly and when young accepted them without question. My father was lord and master of his house – or was he? Was he not a paper tiger that Mother had invented for some subtle reason of her own? He said once that my mother made him an ogre to his children. True, she would say, 'Hush, now, be quiet, Daddy will be home soon and he will be tired after a hard day's work,' and we hushed immediately, but I never heard my father ask us to be quiet. When talking about children with friends he would say, 'You should love 'em and leave 'em alone.' I believe he felt if children were born of healthy and normal parents, they would, because of nature in some way, know what was best for them.

Mother thought it a crime to argue with one's husband in front of the children; for parents to frighten a child by fighting together in that child's presence was to her one of the really wicked things, and she would almost cry out when she heard of little children sitting on the stairs listening to their parents fight. 'It may affect a child all its life,' she would worry. So one of her maxims was, 'It is better to give points away for peace,' but of course she wasn't submissive and by her calm non-acquiescence, I think she *gained* her point. Certainly she loved and admired my father, although sometimes if he grumbled about conditions she would say, 'You are a disappointed man, Walter.' This always infuriated him and he would rub his balding head and grit his teeth and I am sure he would have liked to give Mother a push. I am sure she knew this too, but she still said it and I wonder if she was not really the master of the house. His comfort was her first concern: 'A man must respect himself before he can respect others,' and she would have given her life for him or for her children, yet she was her own woman, always. She felt a woman must always act in a way to command respect from her husband; to be flighty, or allow even one's husband to feel a woman was 'willing', was one sure way of losing a man's respect. It was a man's prerogative to ask; a woman must never, never ask, although it was her duty not to refuse her husband.

It's true my father was a disappointed man, and I suppose neither he nor my mother should have been living in Poplar. They were both intelligent, both having been to school when other children of their ages were sent out to work. I had unusual grandparents in that they paid sixpence a week to send their children to village schools, so that both my parents could write well, had a knowledge of figures and, as my father said, were well versed in 'the three Rs,' although he said this in a sarcastic and humorous way. He did try to retrieve the family fortunes from time to time, but as these ventures all failed, to the amusement of the family, he felt Mother had brain-washed us all to support her and gang up on him.

He was very taken with advertisements in the *News of the World* if they said it was easy to make a fortune in one's spare time. He once saw an advertisement on mushroom-growing and could see the sovereigns rolling in. Much to Mother's silent disgust and pity for his gullibility, he spent all his money on the materials advertised. He was a wonder-ful craftsman, and along the whole length of the backyard he built a wooden growing-box. After much swearing and warnings to the family that, when the magic mushroom loam was planted, the growing-box must not be opened, or even approached, until a certain hour on a certain day, we all waited and waited for the day when the opening ceremony would take place and the Chegwiddens' ship come in.

The great day arrived and we all trooped out eagerly, none so eager or confident as my father. He looked at my mother's unbelieving countenance and shook his head. 'Your mother's never encouraged me,' he said. 'She is an ob-stinate woman who won't ever move with the times.' A sniff from Mother. When we were all present and quiet, with the air of centuries of mushroom-growing in his blood, he threw open the lid of the growing-box. We all believed there would be hundreds and hundreds of Mrs Spink's 'edgicated' mush-rooms with their dear little white elf's roofs. Dead silence, for where the mushrooms should have been were mouse-holes, the whole being covered by a ghostly sheet of filmy cobwebs. Mother turned and walked slowly into the house, Father gazing after her with a look of intense hatred. I really believed it was Mother's fault that the mushrooms had not appeared.

Then all hell broke loose, we all scattered into the house finding various secret corners where we could let loose our hysterical laughter. Mother was under the table shaking and pretending to dust the floor. Someone else was hanging on to the roller-towel in the scullery, and laughter, albeit choked laughter, came from all parts of the house. It was vital we should get it out of our systems before the raging mushroom farmer fell down the back steps. We could all control our-selves when necessary if we didn't look at each other; it was when one of us caught sight of another's eyes that things became dangerous. We all seemed to be reading and en-grossed when Father finally appeared, a beaten man. 'The bloody *News of the World*,' he said. 'It's a put on, and I've a good mind to write to them.'

His next venture was chinchilla rabbits. Fur coats for all

and pelts to sell to the West End. They were such pretty little things and there was so much distress in the family at the time of their death that Father blamed our 'weak stomachs' for the failure of this venture. I believe Marjorie did get a muff out of the chinchilla venture but our disgust at the pelts hanging to dry and our warnings to Marjorie of anthrax and other diseases soon relegated this muff to the dustbin.

A friend of Father's, having a delicate son, decided he would keep chickens: eggs for his son, and eggs to sell to make the family rich. He spent his hard-earned money and time on these chickens, but was unable to stop them from eating their eggs. He was determined to cure these cannibals and he carefully broke eggs, which he bought, filled these eggs with a mustard solution and placed them among the chickens at dead of night. But as soon as the chickens laid a real egg they gobbled it up. He bought some fertile eggs and sat a broody hen on them, but the eggs became addled, the hen having no maternal feelings whatsoever, having eaten as many as she could. He was not going to be done, the thought of his delicate son spurred him on, and he visited Club Row, near Petticoat Lane, and bought some day-old chicks. He nursed them like a mother but they all began to ail and die. He was frantic and made a little coop for them which he covered with wire netting and placed on top of the garden shed in the warm sunshine. Victory was his, for out of the thirteen baby chicks he had purchased, one survived, and it was healthy and chirpy, and this little chick made up for all the heartbreak and expense of the venture. One day the little chick was able to put his head through the wire netting to view the beautiful world for which he had been so carefully nurtured, and the cat next door bit off his head.

As our family began to get older, and even when they were still at home, they pursued their various industrious private lives, so mealtimes became an almost continuous running buffet for Mother. My father always seemed to be having his dinner in solitary state, possibly he arranged this from choice for he always said a lot of women together gave him a headache because they were always 'chewing the bloody fat.' This uncouth expression, which amused the boys, was treated with the ladylike contempt it deserved by the girls and went right over little Marjorie's head, for she began to recite all those members of the family who didn't appreciate fat meat.

It is true he began to enjoy his meals in private, but he couldn't have everything and he often found he was the focal-point for pairs and pairs of intensely staring eyes, for at tea-time, being a working man and the goose which laid the golden eggs (somewhat tarnished eggs, I thought), he was treated to some delicacy which the rest of us had not received. He was fascinating to watch for he ate so differently from Mother. She was never meant by nature to be the poor mother of ten, and the wife of my father, for in everything she did was an inborn deftness and refinement. To see her cut a tomato or peel an apple, or make pastry was a delight, and she ate her meals as I always imagined a queen would eat them, but Father, well . . . The first thing he did when a lovely meal was placed in front of him was to reach for his knife, and like a builder mixing cement he would mix and churn it all up so that it was unrecognisable from the original dish. Stewed cherries and custard would soon become a pink nothingness, and we could never take our eyes off this gourmand. Sometimes he would rub the top of his head uncomfortably and say to Mother, 'Haven't the children had their dinner? Have you given them enough to eat? They are looking at me as though I have robbed them.' But we still continued to gaze at him until he had devoured the last morsel, when he would suck in his moustache and wipe it on the napkin Mother provided for him.

He had two favourite dishes. One was the enormous Cornish pasty Mother would make for him to take to work, and this he called Man Friday's Footprint. He used to say it was the envy of all his mates. The other was curry, and however hot Mother made this curry he always said it wasn't hot enough. He really made this remark from force of habit, like the farmer who once a year closes his footpath to the public. Father had to stress that all was not perfect with Mother or else she might get ideas above her station as a wife, I always thought.

One Saturday we were all at home to dinner together –

with the exception of Father. The others had curry. I detested it, and, to Amy's annoyance, I had something different. Mother said to Amy, 'Well, it's no good giving curry to Dolly, she won't eat it,' but I knew from Amy's look that had she been my mother I would have. Amy loved curry so I thought she might like my share. One and all, without exception, complained that the curry was too hot, and Mother remarked that she was sorry but that it was an ill wind which blew nobody any good and for once Dad would be pleased with the curry. When he finally appeared and sat down to his meal, we all, being sufficiently repleted, began our staring act at our bringer of fertility, waiting for his applause and compliments to the hot curry, knowing this would please Mother. He performed his cement-mixing act. Whether it was the girls' silent disapproval of this I don't know, but after the first mouthful he announced in moaning and irritable tones, 'Just the same as ever, why can't you do as I ask, Mother, and make curry hot; hot, that's what curry is supposed to be.' Our stares turned into looks of amazement as he kept on grumbling.

In the end little Marjorie got up and brought back from the scullery the tin of Eastern Promise, the foreign hot curry powder Mother obtained especially for Father. 'Shake a little bit of this on, Dad, it will mix in, I'm sure.' Father looked at Mother and she looked at him and between them passed one of those looks which only husband and wife can exchange. She was gently smiling her Mona Lisa smile and he knew that she knew he was just being awkward and wouldn't admit that the curry was really hot and really perfect. How could he give in, one against so many? He shook a little of the curry-powder on his dinner and started the cement-mixer in motion again. He had to taste it, and to 'make his own case good' (one of his expressions), he had to shake on a little more to prove Mother wrong. As he shook the tin of curry-powder for the third time, he tapped the bottom of the tin gently (it was nearly full but curry sometimes clings together in a damp sort of way), and the whole contents of the tin poured on to his plate.

A gasp went round the kitchen. Father looked at Mother like a naughty defiant boy and she looked at him with a sweet distant smile, but in that smile was 'and it jolly well serves you right, now eat it if you dare.' Father did dare, and to the horror and admiration of his audience he began to eat 'hot' curry for once. He ate it with great relish as though he had been starving and the delight of delights had been placed before him. Shock spread to the onlookers' surprised faces, for on Father's nose, forehead, cheeks and chin, and even over his bald crown, beads of perspiration began to appear like diamonds. He couldn't mop his brow, for that would have told Mother the curry was too hot, and he slowly finished his meal. With great aplomb or finesse, I thought, he took a piece of bread, gave Mother one pregnant look, and wiped his plate clean, eating this bread very slowly and somewhat painfully. Mother I know was on the point of giggling and we all held our breaths not daring to look at her.

Father got up very slowly and left the room, closing the door behind him; we heard him dash to the scullery sink and turn the tap on and we knew he was drinking pints of water. We then heard him go upstairs, and as we saw him leave the house by the front door, dressed for his club (there was a spy watching for his departure, always) the whole family exploded with a giant burst of laughter. We were all in pain from holding back our laughter in front of Father and two of the boys were rocking on the floor. When the laughter ceased, Mother said sadly, 'I don't suppose Dad will ever ask me to make him curry again, and it's his favourite meal.' The tone of her voice sent us all off again.

There is something very satisfying about being a big frog in a small pond, and my twelfth year was one of my happiest. I convinced myself it was fortunate I had failed the scholarship, for life would have been learning and homework. I would have been one of the masses, whereas now I need do no schoolwork, but just lord it around the school with my little P badge; why, I was as good as a mistress. And in this year, 1923, I had the Christmas of my life, enough joy, I felt, to last me for ever.

Christmas was always a magic time for us, there was a smell in the air quite different from any other season. I had grown out of putting my sock at the end of the bed. After all, what was the point, the fruit we used to find in our socks would be in bowls in the front room now. This special Christmas I had stocked up with books from the library and Mother was busy on Christmas Eve with the usual mincepie making and goose-stuffing. I was glad we had a goose again. The last Christmas we had sat down to an enormous baked rabbit, when it dawned on us all that it was the rabbit from the hutch in the back yard. Father had murdered it and none of us would eat it. I couldn't possibly eat a pet, a friend, and Father had grumbled and sworn that we should all know what it was like to be starving. Mother said he lost his temper because he had a guilty conscience. We never kept a pet rabbit again.

Agnes and Arthur were married, Charlie was a sailor, Winifred was at the bank, Leonard a sailor, Amy in a local office, David at Sir John Cass School, Cecil in an office in Bow, Marjorie and I were at school. This Christmas we would all be together.

The family were all up when lazy Marjorie and I came down to a surprise which made us both speechless. We had never had presents at Christmas and our two places at the table were piled high. Shiny pencil-boxes with flowers on them, pens, pencils, books, red woollen gloves, sweets, a new frock. The whole family gazed and laughed at our faces, and Mother wiped her eyes. She always seemed to me to shed a few tears at the wrong things. I had such a lot of books: *What Katy Did, What Katy Did Next, What Katy Did at School* (I thought perhaps someone thought 'for the want of a nail' might mean something to me). I think Marjorie burst into tears as well.

We spent the afternoon after Christmas dinner going over our presents. I kept wrapping mine up, putting them away in a safe place, then getting them all out again. 'Now, Dolly,' said Mother, 'use them, enjoy them, don't put them away and never have the wear out of them.'

Father was always affable at Christmastime; I loved the smell of his cigar and the way he winked at Mother and me. Meals were never late in our house. My friends had to wait until their fathers came home from the public houses, but my father never went to a public house, he went to his club where they played snooker, skittles, darts, etc., and he always came home for dinner at one o'clock. Tea was at 4.30 and supper at 7.30. I suppose this sticking to routine made my friends sure we were different. But it was lovely for us, especially at Christmastime; we seemed to have hours and hours more time for festivities than my friends, for theirs was a 'hanging-about' time waiting for their fathers. When their mothers were washing up after dinner we had even had Christmas tea and were beginning our fun.

After tea we turned on the gramophone. It was a square mahogany box with a large green horn, and we had records of 'The Laughing Policeman,' Nellie Wallace, George Robey and Dame Clara Butt. As the sailor boys came home from sea more were added to our collection.

It was after tea that the fun started, for my eldest brothers and sisters had invited friends home. We played the writing games first, consequences, and of course, my favourite, towns, countries, rivers. There was always much argument as to which letter we would use each time, and usually Winnie settled this by taking the first letter on the page from a book she would open at random. Great cries if she hit on the same letter twice in a row. The game went on for some time, usually ending when the arguments got too fierce and the answers could not be checked in the huge dictionary Winnie had won at George Green's School.

Having got the guests appreciably settled, Father would disappear downstairs to his barrel and his Zane Grey or Jack London book, and now the celebrations really began. The whole family, except myself, did a turn. Agnes told a sad story, Arthur sang 'The Cornish Floral Dance' in a sort of quavering baritone (I felt shy and wouldn't look at him). Charlie played the mandoline, Amy frightened us all with the 'Green Eye of the Little Yellow God,' and at the applause, which was exceptional and meant, to Amy, an encore, she began 'Lascar' by Alfred Noyes. But whoever was master of ceremonies cut this encore short as there were many more performers yet. Not like me, Amy thought. I think she was right, and I was always jealous of her dramatic bent and lovely voice. David told a few jokes at which the boys screamed and Mother tutted. Cecil sang a song, for he had been in the church choir.

I did nothing and no one pressed me about this. By tacit consent there was really nothing Dolly could do, and little Marjorie, who had left the room, now returned dressed in a sort of pale green rag. She was to do her nymph's dance, of which she was the sole proud performer and choreographer. Mother always gazed very fondly and proudly at Marjorie as she cavorted round the room in bare feet, gazing into the woods and ferns of nymphland, and we all clapped Marjorie very loudly. I admired her for her bravery and was also jealous of her achievement. She was very pretty and always chosen for the princess or heroine in the school plays when I was the old wicked king, or Scrooge. Amy said I should take that as a compliment, but I would much rather have been the beautiful heroine.

None of the guests performed. 'We would rather enjoy watching,' they all said politely. Then we had games. Snap-apple: with such a crowd of people the apples had constantly to be restrung, but Mother had set aside the round ones with strong stalks before Christmas. Snap-apple was taken in turns by seniority so I came after Cecil, which was not nice in one way for, always so vicious to the apple and determined to split it, he usually split his lip instead, so the apple had little flecks of Cecil's blood on it when it came to my turn, but of course through Cecil's vigour I achieved a bit, then I received my applause of the evening.

We played Family Coach, where Arthur told such a wonderful tale that most of us were caught, so engrossed were we with his story. We put the Tail on the Donkey, Mother loved that game. We played All Birds Fly, and laughed when one of the guests raised his hand at 'elephants fly.' It took ages for everybody to do their forfeits. And there were the super games where you can catch people who haven't played the game, and so it was lovely to have guests, for sometimes they knew games we didn't and vice versa.

This Christmas we played Confessions. Arthur dressed up as a clergyman and in his flat country vicar's hat he balanced a large amount of water. As each person entered the room he had to kneel in front of the priest and confess his sins, and when the priest bent to give him absolution so of course he would be soaked with water. Mother insisted each sinner wear a thick towel round his shoulders, for this game worried her. Arthur told the absolution-seekers the towel was the confessional surplice. Cecil's friend brought the house down because, not knowing the game, he confessed he had been extra sinful and had stolen Aldgate Pump.

We played silent charades, acting charades; Amy and I got together on charades, for it was our favourite game of the evening. I had the good ideas and she could act so perfectly.

In one way Christmas was marred for Winnie, but she never let it rankle. She had wanted a pair of brown boots all her life. Mother had said, when Winifred was little, and pleaded for these brown boots, 'When you grow up and go out to work you will be able to buy a pair of brown boots, but you will never be able to buy another stomach.' Mother couldn't manage two pairs of boots for Winnie and she had to wear black for school. Well, Winifred had now bought these brown boots, the best quality obtainable, but she had got them soaking wet in the rain, and Mother suggested she place them in the oven by the side of the kitchen fire at night when she went to bed; the warmth remaining in the oven after the fire was out would gently dry the boots.

Alas, many fires were lit before Winnie remembered the boots. Mother drew them from the oven with a cloth because they were so hot. We all looked at Winnie for the boots were perfect pantomime boots and could have done service for a male comic or an Arabian magician. Mother started to laugh, she tried not to, but the boots were so comical and Winnie's face so unusually tragic and out of character, that what with the glass of port wine Father had given us all, even Marjorie and me (well, ours were little glasses), and the boys laughing, Winnie began to whoop with the rest of us. We were calm again until Mother said, 'It was so strange. All the week I kept smelling something and couldn't trace it,' and we all thought of Father's banished boots at no. 13, and off we all went again.

The oven beside the fire caught Mother out many times, for in a hot summer she would put the butter in the oven, it was cool there, and Father often lit a fire on a summer evening, he always felt the cold. The butter was never thought about until it ran out all oily. Mother was often caught out with her puddings too. Christmas puddings needed hours and hours of boiling and Mother made so many she often went to bed tired and left the puddings boiling with a note to the last one in either to change the puddings over, or to turn the gas out, for we had a gas stove now. Each older member of the family carried out Mother's instructions and the puddings all had to be boiled again for Mother never knew which ones had been changed or not. Father thought women stupid and disorganised, but Mother never knew which member of the family would arrive home last, and so she couldn't put the name on the note. It was arranged in the end that the one who changed the puddings over should write on the note. No one made puddings like Mother and she would not put the mixture in the basins until every member of the family had stirred the stiff mixture and wished. These wishes we all took seriously and knew they would come true, but we little ones had a job to stir the stiff rich-smelling mixture and Mother had to help us.

We never minded going to bed on Christmas night, for one thing we were tired, and for another we had Boxing Day to look forward to. In our house it was Christmas Day all over again.

12 **Purely platonic**

Joining the public library was a red-letter day for me. It was one department then with no books for small children. Choosing a book was a difficult task for a beginner, for books were entered in catalogues under code numbers, long numbers they seemed to me. Hundreds of corresponding numbers were displayed behind the glass windows on the library walls. There were never enough catalogues and much time was spent in waiting one's turn for a catalogue. Then having chosen a book the glass windows would have to be searched for the number. If the number was blue, one was in luck, but if red, the book was out, and back to the catalogue which of course someone else had then, always such a slow person it seemed to me. At first I did not understand the catalogues, and my reading consisted of *Mistress of the Upper Sixth, Fifth Form at St . . ., Terror of the School*, until I discovered different authors. I left my normal world and lived in a world of fantasy. I was deaf to all other sounds and Mother sometimes got cross because I would not put my book down for one moment. We had possessed one dog-eared book that all the family had read and cried over. *Froggie's Little Brother*.

Froggie and his little brother were orphans living in a garret. Froggie had scoured the streets for a crust of bread. His little brother was dying and one knew it wouldn't be long before Froggie, too, breathed his last. He found a stale crust of bread in the gutter and was feeding it to his little brother to save his life, when out of the wainscotting came their only friend in life, a mouse; this friend too was starving and with great emotion Froggie's little brother said, 'Feed the mouse.' One knew as the mouse was eating this rich repast, Froggie's little brother would gasp his last, followed by a slow dying Froggie. At this point my sobs became uncontrollable.

Mother thought she had got used to this torture with my eight brothers and sisters, but my broken heart was one to beat all others and one day she snatched the book from me and fed it to the copper fire fearing I would make myself ill.

Now Mother would be unable to treat the library books in this fashion, for defilement was not allowed and a punishable offence. We read at school, of course, but this was not a real pleasure, for all reading was aloud and as we read paragraphs in turn one had to keep pace with the slowest reader. Many times I tried to dash on secretly, but I could never keep the place in the book with my finger and was always being called out to read; being so many pages ahead, I was unable to discover where the previous girl had left off, to the anger of the teacher. I used to pray they would have examinations in silent reading.

I was very worried about the library fines; if I incurred them, no one at home would pay them and I dreaded what I would do and of course in addition I would be expelled from the library. I read my books on a clean piece of rag and always washed my hands first. One day I rested my book on the scullery table while I went to the shops for Mother. When I returned, the precious book had been knocked down by the side of the parrot's cage and the parrot had devoured a third of the thick cover all down the longest edge of the book. It was a tragedy. I should have taken care of it. I went to the library a broken woman. It was impossible to hide the damage but I still had to go on, for they might send an inspector, I thought, if the book became overdue. Amy had asked me to get her a book, any romance would do. I did not know the young assistant was sweet on Amy and I asked him for a book on love. He asked if it was for Amy and I said, Yes, and I handed him my half-eaten book and he said he was sorry it had been given to me like that! I thought a miracle had happened. I wasn't expelled and I wasn't fined. When I told Amy I had asked for her book on love and the assistant had said she would enjoy the one on love he had specially chosen for me, Amy said, 'Oh, Dolly, whatever made you mention that word to *him*?' I couldn't see what I had done wrong, but I was glad I had used that word and I forgave the parrot.

I would start reading my book as I left the library. One day there was a terrific wind behind me and an almighty noise as though all the wooden shutters had fallen down from all the shops, and something slid down my back and I stumbled forward. A man came up and told me to run home to Mother quickly. A woman had jumped from the top of a high building as I passed and missed me by a fraction of an inch. A miracle, everyone told Mother. I said I thought the woman should have looked before she leapt and she would have seen me walking underneath. Mother said, 'Poor distracted woman, if she had looked, perhaps she wouldn't have jumped.' I felt sick.

Twice after that I walked under the heads of cart-horses while reading, and the order went out from home that I must not read while walking in the street. Ever after I ran all the way home.

All my sisters had best friends at this time, and I longed for one too. One of Amy's 'sisters under the skin' affairs was with a girl called Pearl Hillside. To start with what a beautiful name, Pearl, that glowing, gleaming gem, like cool, clear water, and Hillside, that never ending rise of beautiful green slopes and snowy peaks.

Pearl Hillside lived with her mother who was a widow. Her father had died it was said, with the consumption and Mother didn't really like Amy going to play at Pearl's house because of the terrible galloping germs that would surely be lurking there, but Amy, always obdurate, often escaped to this lovely place. Pearl's uncle was an estate agent, as I remember, and they lived on one of the floors above the 'shop,' a sort of grace and favour residence. I believe they had a lodger and Amy and Pearl had to play quietly in the afternoons because Pearl's mother and the lodger were resting, contemplating the mountain and Mahomet, perhaps. The mother must have been tired for she cleaned the offices there. She was beautifully dressed in the latest fashion and she dressed Pearl in the same elegant way. Amy worshipped all this. Pearl's mother at one time wore widow's weeds, the smartest weeds ever seen in any pond. The flowing black veil, gloves, jet beads, black silk stockings, tight-waisted gown, beautiful black-buttoned boots, were something to behold, especially when she was followed by Pearl, also elegantly and adultly attired in this sombre colour, but of course it wasn't sombre, it was really startling.

Outside in the yard was a corrugated tin shed on which Amy built a house. She cooked gooseberries over a fire and was proud when they turned out like Mother's. Pearl didn't want to do any of these things but Amy was the dominant partner. She just loved Pearl and all the appurtenances of her family and they were left to their own devices a lot for the mother was always off somewhere.

Amy would squeeze Pearl and hold her hand, just because she thought she possessed such a beautiful friend who loved her and had such an exciting place to live in with these ravishing clothes, but even a worm will turn, and one day the blow fell. Amy received from Pearl her first and last letter. 'Dear Amy, I cannot be friends with you any more because you are too pashonate.' Amy was heartbroken, but also very, very puzzled, and so were we all, for neither Amy nor the family knew what Pearl meant by 'pashonate.' Anyway Mother was greatly relieved because of the 'consumption' which might have galloped into our house. 'Everything happens for the best,' she told a weeping Amy. But how can one believe even such a truthful person as one's mother when the future was black and, for Amy, so flat without the Hillsides?

Mother had a Jewish friend, Annie, a dark-haired lady who would bring us sheets of hard biscuits with little holes in them. I couldn't stop eating them but Mother said they would dry up my blood. Mother was very proud of having Annie come to see us. She said if a Jewish person is your friend, you have a friend for life. Therefore I thought I must try to get a Jewish friend. This was difficult for there were no Jewish people living in Poplar, that I knew of. They only had shops or stalls in Chrisp Street. We had one Jewish girl in my class, but there was the problem of her name, which was a pity for she was always so nice to me and would have made a lovely bosom pal. Her name was Selina Lipshitz, but the teacher never even liked to say her name and always called her, very firmly and obviously so we wouldn't be mistaken, 'Lipsips.' So I couldn't take such a name home if even the teacher couldn't speak it because it was rude. Therefore I had to look further afield.

I passed another Jewish girl on my way to school. She looked about my age and I thought this was the answer to my problem, and every day I looked hard at her so that one day we could become friends. Mother said everybody took to us, so I knew it was only a matter of time before this girl I passed took to me. I looked for her every morning and afternoon. One day she was with another girl and as I approached she came over to me and I thought we were going to start our friendship, but she shouted, 'What do you keep bossing at me for, moggy four-eyes?' I was terrified. This wasn't the beginning of a life-long friendship and loyalty on her part, it was the opening for battle. I turned and ran home to Mother and told her all about it, and she said, 'Well, now Marjorie is growing up, you will have her for a friend.' So I had Marjorie, but I didn't tell Mother Marjorie was a sister. How could she be my bosom friend?

Mother had another friend who used to visit, but I wouldn't have wanted her for a bosom friend for she was a granny. I don't know where she came from but we called her Mrs Walker. Like all grannies she wore a flat high hat, like a rounded kettle-holder, tied under her chin with velvet and edged with jet beads, a rusty cape with the same beaded border, a voluminous skirt, elastic-sided boots and she carried a little Dorothy bag. This was a sort of grannie's uniform. She trembled permanently and my brothers always waited excitedly for her to upset her tea. She would always nod trembling towards Amy and pronounce, 'Her's the fairest of them all.' Since Amy was dark I thought granny

Walker was so old she had forgotten the difference between dark and fair, or she was colour blind.

Mother said sadly that children were children for such a short time, and she would have liked to keep us always young, I felt. But when her sister Annie from Dorset 'braved the dangers of London, the robbers and cut-throats' (this amused us), and visited Mother with Cousin Fred, she was proud of her growing-up family, for now only four, two boys and two girls, were not at work, engaged, or married. Mother and Auntie Annie hadn't seen each other for years and they sat side by side, and held hands. Cousin Fred's life-long ambition was to visit Petticoat Lane. Auntie Annie was terrified for him; 'Thou must not go, Snow.' Mother laughed when I asked why Cousin Fred was always called Snow. It was 'thouest know.' Cousin Fred did visit that resort with his little leather purse. Father said he came back with a bargain pair of checked woollen trousers, discovering on arrival home that these bargains had been made for a man with one wooden leg. I think Father was teasing us. Auntie Annie persuaded Dad to take a holiday with Mother's brother Arthur who lived in a farmhouse in Romsey in Hampshire, and Mother was as excited as a child. There was much swearing from Father, already regretting his weakness to Auntie Annie in promising such an expedition, and we all set off. Father even took black Nugget polish for his boots, and on Waterloo station the case burst, scattering the contents, more swearing and raging, so that we finally got on to the train with lots of clothes in our arms.

It was the loveliest holiday I had ever had, and I preferred the country to the sea. We had been to Folkestone when I was younger for Father had gone to an army camp there. We had rooms with a Mrs Fawcett. Mother gave her money for food each day but was sure that this landlady bought margarine and charged for butter. Mother detested margarine. The beach was all stones which hurt my feet and I got sunstroke and spent my holiday painfully in bed with bright red curtains in the tiny bedroom through which the sun continually poured.

It was different at Uncle Arthur's. He was a very kind and gentle man, who watched Mother with brotherly affection, delighting in her laughter. His wife was a very strong man/woman, with men's laceless boots. She was silent, but jolly, and bathed us all in the barn, with much laughter, in an enormous round wooden tub. She didn't pat us when she dried us, as Mother did, but rubbed us down with great vigour. She brushed my hair with long hard strokes and my head seemed to go back to my waist. I think she was used to grooming the horses on the farm, and she loved brushing my hair so much I thought she would never stop, and I would never get my head upright again. She asked me if I would like to live on the farm with her and Uncle Arthur for always, but I said, not without my mother, and she tickled me until I gasped for breath. She was a strong loving woman.

Mother took us along the hedgerows and knew the names of every flower, bird and tree. She saw wild strawberries where we couldn't and said we had 'town eyes.' She was like a girl she was so happy. My dad spent the holiday in his best suit, flushed, tottery and happy, although one tragedy marred the lovely holiday. We had found a tiny bird with its wing broken and feeling so miserable decided to put it in with the chickens, sure that they would mother it until it could fly again. Carefully we opened the door to the chickens' run, tenderly we placed the little bird inside, and the chickens came screaming and half-flying to tear this little bird to pieces in front of our terrified eyes. The chickens were like eagles with their wild screams, threshing talons and beaks. Our screams brought Mother running and she cried, and said why didn't we wait and ask her about the little bird. Sadly she said it was nature's way, the law of the jungle, and Father said, 'Big fleas have little fleas.' We didn't know what he meant and thought secretly it was the country cider making him say strange things.

The following year Winnie became engaged, and as her fiancé was at sea most of the time, she was preparing her bottom drawer and couldn't mix with other young men; it was a time to be faithful; her ring with the diamonds was a constant reminder she was 'spoken for.' It was a lovely time for Marjorie and me, for Winnie took us out every week-end. We went to Greenwich where we saw Queen Elizabeth's bath and she (Winnie, not Queen Elizabeth) rolled down the hills with us and we thought of the time when Mother had taken us all out on picnics there, and we tried to read the 24-hour clock and watch the red ball go up on the observatory. Mother used to take an enormous cold rice pudding in her enamel pie-dish. Sometimes Mother had taken us to Victoria Park; that was quite an expedition for we would have to go by train from Poplar station. It was only one station away, but it was a real exciting train journey. We would argue about which was the best carriage, and finally all pile in, and when the guard waved his green flag we would all sing.

Winnie took us further afield, to London, and to Richmond where lived a cousin Trudy. She owned a Tea Shoppe with little bottle-glass windows and I was upset when Winnie refused Trudy's offer of a nice meal. I thought grown-ups were strange in their refusals of such lovely things and I was tired and had a blister on my foot. I lost my little Sunday handbag and Winnie said, 'Don't cry, I will take you to Scotland Yard where all lost things are sent.' First of all she took me to a man's shop near Scotland Yard and bought me a little round beaver hat, just like the bank manager's daughters wore, and so the policeman called me miss when I told him what my little bag contained. 'One piece of rag, ironed by mother to look like a hankie, two texts, one of the baby Jesus and one of the three wise men, a farthing, and a spare gob.' This last was a perfect round stone I had found and so was an extra to my set of 'bonce and gobs.'

We went to Wales to meet Winnie's future in-laws. They lived in a village about eighteen miles from Cardiff and kept an inn. The inn had a yard attached to it where the farmers from the hills brought their cattle, horses, and pigs to sell on

Mondays, and the inn was full of smoke and red-faced men talking a foreign language and laughing very loudly. I was too young to go into the bars but I could see them from the kitchen, and on Mondays there was a constant stream of tottering red-faced foreigners staggering to the men's lavatory. Further down the passage inside a shed in the garden was the ladies' lavatory for it had two black holes in a white scrubbed box and a smaller hole in a lower box. I was horrified at this. I thought a family of Welsh people would descend on me *en masse*, for there was no lock on the door. At home it was considered not the thing if one member of the family should hurry another up even in an emergency. I was frightened of the black bottomless pit and was sure some monster would come up from the depths and either bite my bottom or attach itself to my nether portions. Mother laughed when I told her of my distaste for country lavatories, for someone she knew in her childhood days fixed his family lavatory on his vegetable garden to fertilise the crops. This was the end for me and I wondered why the man and his family weren't poisoned when they ate vegetables.

We picked watercress from the stream in Wales and I wished Mother could have some instead of having to pay for it in Chrisp Street. The Welsh girls were beautiful with lovely pink-and-white skins. I never knew girls could have such lovely complexions, but their perfection was marred, for me, for I thought they had rather thick ankles. My father said it was through climbing the Welsh hills. It was the first time I had seen ants, and Winnie's future mother-in-law thought I was a funny London girl because I wouldn't eat her lovely Welsh cakes. She had to bang them first to shake off the ants. But suppose I thought an ant was a currant and swallowed it!

13 **Almost a saint**

The parish church was the centre of our family's social activities. My brothers belonged to the boys' club and took their turns as choirboys, and Cecil pumped the organ. Amy and Winnie were guides, Agnes belonged to the girls' club, Agnes did exhibitions with clubs and dumb-bells, Amy did exhibitions with a skipping-rope. It was fantastic to see them. I thought I could do fancy skipping, but I hoped no one would ask me to swing the clubs for I was sure to send one spinning across the hall to knock poor old Sister Kathleen's head off. She looked after the church with Sister Annie. It was painful to meet Sister Kathleen. She had long bony fingers; she would place her forefinger forcefully in the cavity in my neck, holding my cheek from the mouth up very firmly between two other bony digits. Then she would ply me with questions about my dear mother and my lovely brothers and sisters. Since what I answered was unintelligible and the position of my mouth always caused me to dribble, I could never understand why she seemed delighted with my answers. My brother, Arthur, once told Sister Kathleen, when she had been describing the sewing-machine, that modern innovation, that his mother could sew faster than any machine, and she repeated this remark constantly all the years I knew her.

We had various curates come and go while I attended the church, all lovely young men, all aristocratic, and so the maidens at the church were in a permanent state of being in love with one or other of them.

We had, as a rule, thin serious rectors, and I preferred them serious, although we had a very fat jolly one once, like Edward Arnold the film star. So it was a sad shock for us all when he drank a bottle of carbolic acid one night on

Hackney marshes. 'Many a brave smiling face hides a sad heart,' Mother said, and I was fearful for her for a long time.

Then we had Mr Evans, the curate everybody loved. He worked tirelessly for the church and for the poor. He started boys' clubs, men's clubs, women's and girls'. We all wanted to do our best for Mr Evans. Amy always seemed to be blotting her copybook and was upset as she valued his good opinion.

Mr Evans held a concert for our local church talent. Everyone was there. Len was sitting behind Amy larking about with his friends. Amy, perhaps a little nervous at her forthcoming recitation, boxed Len's ears, just as Mr Evans entered. 'Amy, Amy,' he said reproachfully, and poor Amy wanted to die of shame, or execute Len. Mr Evans called Len up first to open the concert. 'A sea shanty, sung by Leonard Chegwidden,' announced Mr Evans. A red-faced Len started by inhaling all the air in the hall at one go. 'One Friday morn when we set sail our ship across the bay – phew,' a mighty exhalation of Len's remaining wind and the sad words, 'I'm sorry I can't do any more.' Mr Evans helped an exhausted Len off the stage. Amy recited 'Barbara Freitchie' and the whole audience clapped so much she gave an encore. I was to sing, with Geraldine Fisher, 'Won't you come and play in my back yard,' and I was dressed up in gingham, which I detested, for the occasion. Geraldine had recently come to the district. Her parents were old music-hall entertainers, and this concert could have been the opportunity for their daughter to be recognised. For weeks they had trained us, well Geraldine really, for she was a real trouper, had no shyness, and possessed a voice. I never knew what voice I possessed, I couldn't make out whether it was low, or high, or a musical speaking one.

The pianist started and so did Geraldine. When I should have come in I was still not sure what voice to use, so sometimes I sang low, sometimes high, sometimes in the middle. To my horror the whole hall was hysterical. Geraldine never spoke to me again. I felt ashamed and Dad's friend told him

I was as good as Nellie Wallace. I did not need this insult to stop me from entertaining in public, or private, again.

We had Sunday school teas, yellow cake and watery tea, and we took our own cups. We went to Theydon Bois for an outing one summer, and, the first time I saw the sea, we went to Southend. Sister Kathleen was loaded with new clothes for children who would, of course, fall into the sea, and many of the children came back better dressed than when they went.

When Marjorie joined the guides, Mother, feeling sorry perhaps that she wouldn't allow me to be a guide, said I could join the King's Messengers, a sort of new kind of Band of Hope which the new curate had started. He was a refined, fair young man, intent on helping the poor, but I think the East End had been a bigger shock to him than he had bargained for because he had a dazed look about him. He was very earnest and sincere and on our first evening at King's Messengers (it was $\frac{1}{2}$d. per month) as the membership cards had not arrived, he said we would all chat and get to know one another. He chatted for a while with dead silence from the would-be messengers. Then he said, 'Shall we tell some funny stories?' My friends were delighted, but my heart sank, I was forever afraid we would be shown up in front of the upper classes. He told a few funny stories at which no one laughed, which puzzled him a bit, then seeing my friend, Lizzie, Lizzie of the hoarse voice, eagerly fidgeting, he said, 'I believe dear Lizzie has a really good story for us, let's all pay attention and listen to Lizzie.'

Little Lizzie started and I dreaded to hear the end of the story, knowing Lizzie. Her story was the one where two old ladies are sitting on a tram when along comes a man with a donkey-barrow full of peas. One old lady remarks she hasn't had a pea for years and the barrow man says, 'Gee-up, Neddy, there's going to be a flood.' The curate was shocked to the core. Such a story at King's Messengers. Then Lizzie, no one could stop her now, said, 'The tram-driver can say, all those who can't swim, please go on top.' The curate swallowed and said, 'Yes, well, perhaps we will leave early tonight as it is our first night,' and we ended with a prayer. Lizzie laughed all the way out of the hall and went off down the street laughing. Disgusted with my friend I ran home to tell Mother. She laughed and said she didn't think the curate would have a story night again.

Later when I was to be confirmed by the Bishop of Stepney and was beginning to be a saint – I know I looked like one and tried to behave like one – Cecil became a problem. He was in the choir and was a giggler, it didn't need much to start him laughing, and he complained to Mother that I made him laugh in church when I genuflected low before entering the pew and then looked at him with a very solemn face. Then all his friends would start too and the choirmaster had to read the riot act to them. I was ordered by Mother to sit at the back of the church far away from the choir stalls; I did this obediently but I sat at the end of the pew near the aisle and when I knew the choir was approaching I would innocently turn round and look at Cecil, and he still started to giggle at me, but Mother had nowhere else to banish me to.

Sister Annie took me for confirmation classes and taught me the catechism. I learnt the ten commandments religiously for I remembered what happened to Amy when she attended confirmation classes. The Sister then in charge was very, very old, very, very bent, with a permanent shake and a deep man's voice and craggy face I found frightening. She would call out the number of a commandment and wait for a girl to recite the correct commandment. The only one Amy had learnt was 'Thou shalt not commit adultery.' She knew neither the number nor the meaning of this commandment, so that whatever number the sister called out, Amy recited in her loud voice, 'Thou should not commit adultery.' She knew she would have to be right once out of ten; Sister's stern admonishment for Amy to be silent each time she was wrong made no difference to the eager Amy, determined to shine on at least one commandment. Finally the ancient virgin's righteous indignation at Amy's insistence on this terrible recital was brought to breaking-point and

Amy was dismissed from the class. Arriving home in disgrace Mother tutted at Amy's brazen demeanour which Father thought comical, and so I was very careful to learn all the commandments with their appropriate numbers. I thought I should finally be turned into a saint when the bishop laid his hands on me, but nothing happened. I heard no voice calling me to Him and I felt I had been let down. Marjorie heard beautiful music when the bishop laid his hands on her head, and I felt quite envious of her state of grace.

I must have been a little saintlike though, for I was chosen to be a Sunday school teacher in the little kindergarten and I told the children lovely bible stories. One day the superintendent was away and I had to take the collection. This was then taken to the church and blessed at the evening service with the adult collection. I didn't do very well, perhaps the little children thought I was not a real grown-up, no one to be afraid of, and they didn't put their money in the little velvet bag I passed among them. It had a gold cross embroidered on it. The collection came to $3\frac{1}{2}$d., and I got reading after Sunday school and forgot to take it to church that evening. It remained in my bedroom and I borrowed a penny from it for something or other, knowing Winnie would give me a penny to replace it for the following Sunday's blessing. Mother found the collection bag, this holy receptacle, in my bedroom, was horrified it should be there at all, more horrified I had borrowed from it. 'Those who go a-borrowing, go a-sorrowing,' she said sternly to me, frightening me very much for I hadn't borrowed human money but holy gold. She put the penny in and I was despatched to the rectory, trying to make up a story about the delay which would ring true. The maid showed me into the waiting-room at the rectory and I enjoyed the time I had to wait, for the rector was having a musical evening and the strains on the cello were lovely and sad. I think he was annoyed about being dragged away in the middle of the recital, and I somehow don't think he believed my story, and he looked a little aghast at the size of the collection.

A little while before I was due to leave school, Sister Kathleen asked Mother to bring me to a garden party which was to be held in the grounds of the rectory. A gentleman from the City was to open the fete and Sister Kathleen wanted to introduce us to him for she felt, indeed she had no doubt, that my bright and smiling countenance and Mother's ladylike appearance would ensure for me a situation in the City gentleman's firm. In addition to my cheerful face I was of course, sober, respectable, and most important, Church of England. The joint belief of Sister Kathleen and my mother, that a wonderful future was assured for me, was not, however, shared by me. I felt it was a pity that I had been in the school choir solely because of the winning smile Miss Wilkie asserted I possessed, for it seemed I was being compelled to wear a fixed grin when at heart I felt depressed and unsure of myself.

Adult confidence in me only made me feel more certain I was incapable. It was assumed that the larger and poorer a family, the tougher, less sensitive, are its members, not only because they had learned to share everything, but also because the home truths administered by brothers and sisters automatically knocked off all prickly corners. Outwardly I may have appeared as confident as the rest of the family but inwardly I possessed an inferiority complex because I knew I was inferior. Supposed compliments dished out to me by family and friends, intended to bolster me up, were delivered in such a way as to cast me further down. While I was reading they would say 'The trouble with Dolly is...' or, 'Funny, I never noticed before that Dolly's hair is golden in the sun,' or 'At least Dolly has good ankles,' so these remarks, prefaced as they were with suspect words, I took for condolences, and became more despondent and inwardly nervous.

Mother decided I should have a new dress for my coming out and Miss Cook made me a special one for the occasion. It was cream silk with cream georgette sleeves. I didn't like the shape of the frock for it was low-waisted, if waist was the right word, for the wide sash was just about crutch level and to make matters worse in the centre at the front of the sash was a large rose, made of the silk material. This rose Miss Cook had corded and it was much admired by Mother. The large full georgette sleeves, tight at the embroidered cuffs, I thought were very beautiful and romantic. Of course, for a garden party, a hat must be worn, and that was where the difficulty would arise, for everyone agreed, 'Dolly hasn't got a hat face.' My sisters could look attractive even in the little egg-cosies they knitted in one evening. When I tried any of these on even Mother laughed and Father rubbed his head. But Mother was sure somewhere there was a hat to suit Dolly, and Marjorie was despatched with me to purchase and seek this creation. She was truthful and sensible, and we would arrive home with this crowning glory.

The Poplar shops were unable to accommodate me, one assistant remarking sourly that if none of the hats in her shop suited me I wouldn't get a hat anywhere. Mother was so determined I should be successful that she despatched us to Lewisham where there was a magnificent store. 'Why,' said Mother, 'the gentry shop there.'

The Lewisham store had large and heavy swing doors. These appeared to close, then suddenly exuded a noisy hiss, giving an unwary customer a firm push in the back. Standing outside these swing doors when we arrived was a tiny old lady. She wasn't wearing the usual black granny uniform but we could tell she was as old as a granny in her little metal-framed spectacles. She was dressed in a large coarse grey type of army greatcoat which almost reached the pavement and nearly covered her tiny buttoned boots. Her grey hand-knitted hat, with a large black button at each side, was like an upturned rowing-boat, and as she wore this sideways on her head I thought she looked like a miniature Napoleon, but Marjorie whispered to me that the old lady must be an orphan. I would have told Marjorie that all very old ladies were orphans, but I didn't want to upset Marjorie for she was to help me buy a hat.

We pushed open the heavy doors by concerted effort and the old lady trotted with us to the hat department where the kind assistant offered to leave us to choose a hat by ourselves. She stationed herself a short way from us but assumed an athletic pose, ready to dash forward when we had made our choice which she seemed to assume would be a rapid one. But each hat I tried on made me feel more depressed and Marjorie and the old lady more hysterical, although they both tried to hide their amusement from me. Whenever I became suicidally miserable some quirk in my nature always came to my aid and put a comical thought into my mind. When Marjorie passed me an enormous black shiny hat my first reaction was that it was a fireman's helmet and that it had got into the hat department by mistake, for it had a band round the crown with a large brass buckle, a large brim back and front and no brim on either side. The finishing touch was a long chin strap also completed with a large gold buckle. I tried on this huge black shiny hat which came down over my face and turning to little 'orphan Annie', I said, 'Keep the fire going until I get there.' Marjorie crossed her legs like a pantomime horse and started to bleat like a goat, the old lady's teeth fell down and she shook like a little skeleton; putting out a hand to steady herself she knocked over a hat stand on which was displayed a beautiful pink creation crowned by a bird of paradise. The assistant advanced menacingly, aghast at my dreadful and unmannerly behaviour. What would Mother say? I ordered Marjorie to take the old lady's arm and we made our way hurriedly from the store.

It was some time before I could calm Marjorie and the little old lady. We saw the old lady across the road and waved to her until she was out of sight. As we walked to the bus we were very worried at what Mother would say when we arrived home without the hat she was eagerly awaiting. In this desperate state we espied in the window of a tiny draper's shop, a cream straw hat. Its brim was turned up on one side and edged with brown ribbon. As it was the colour of my new dress I went in and tried it on. It was pronounced 'ladylike' by Marjorie, this would please Mother, and so we bought it. It cost 2s. 11¾d. and so we also had a packet of pins to bring home to Mother. She said 'h'mm' when I tried on the hat at home, and David said it was the shape of the dustman's hat.

On the Saturday afternoon of the garden party I repaired to my bedroom to make myself into a lady. I left off my woollen combinations because they would have shown through the lovely georgette sleeves of the frock. After examining myself from all angles in the mottled swing mirror on the chest of drawers (I thought my arms showing through the georgette sleeves, the most beautiful I had ever seen), I walked slowly and gracefully down the stairs to receive Mother's approval, which I was sure would be ecstatic. Therefore I was unprepared for her look of horror and disgust, and all because I had removed my woollen combinations. I was 'almost naked,' she insisted sternly. After arguing with Mother until she lost her temper I went upstairs in a fearful rage and put the wretched combinations on again. The elbow length sleeves looked dreadful under the beautiful georgette but Mother said my arms were now much more ladylike and so we set off, me with the sulks, no winning smile which was to obtain for me a wonderful situation in life. Mother had a beautiful tricorne straw hat in which she looked lovely, but having rushed to prepare tea for the rest of the family, and after experiencing such a tremendous argument with me, she hurriedly got ready and in her haste and upset hadn't realised she was wearing her hat sideways. I was so full of my own misery that I hadn't even looked at her garden party ensemble.

The anti-climax came when Sister Kathleen sadly informed us the City gentleman had had to rush abroad, and when we arrived home again the family became hysterical at the sight of Mother's hat. Mother said irritably, 'That's Dolly's fault. I don't know what I can do about her.' Then she added that she realised now why the Vicar kept laughing at her. Someone had taken a snap of Mother and me at the garden party. My woollen sleeves showed through the dress and Mother's hat looked as though it had been put on her head after a drunken brawl. I asked her if I should tear up the photograph, and she gave me a hug and said, 'Yes,' which was her way of telling me that georgette sleeves do look better on top of bare arms. I always wished I could have a hat face.

14 A stylish marriage

At about the time I left school my sister Winnie got married. I was happy for her, but sad for myself, for she was going to live right up in the bush in Australia and I was sure I would never see her again. I looked forward to the wedding for I thought it would be a grand affair in the church hall, as Winnie and her husband-to-be were grammar school graduates – he had been a private scholar at a very exclusive establishment in Wales. He was an officer in the Merchant Navy and Winnie's office colleagues who would be coming to the wedding were girls who didn't *have* to go out to work. They lived in places like Kensington and St John's Wood. One of them even owned a dog with a pedigree, and he had papers to prove it, and his name was Cayley Pop Off. I was a human and I only had a very small birth certificate. Winnie's office friends all had boys' nicknames and I thought it was either because they had no brothers or because they were 'pin money' girls.

Winnie's future in-laws were all coming up from Wales and I imagined it would be, for Poplar, a society wedding with me an important bridesmaid. Alas, shock number one; Winnie decided, very sensibly thought Mother, to save the expense of a big white wedding with bridesmaids. It was more important to consider her future needs in a new country. She then decided to hold the reception at home, then the biggest shock of all to me, but applauded by the others, Winnie said as the weather was so hot she would have her wedding breakfast in our back yard. 'But the lavatory is there,' I said to my father. 'Quite a convenience,' he chuckled. 'We can pop in and pop out.'

Mother always thought I was discontented, 'agin the government,' or ashamed of my home. It was none of these things. Had it just been the family and local friends I would have been as happy as the rest of the family, but the thought of people from a different world coming to see what the others ignored, to me was agony. Winnie said 'My friends come to visit me, not my surroundings.' All Winnie's friends were middle class and Mother said proudly, 'Once any of them come here, they enjoy themselves so much they all want to come again.' This was true and they were all such lovely girls, I had to admit that. But I remember how I hated the 'charabangs' which drove round the East End in the summer months loaded with tourists and a guide gazing with fright at the slums. My father used to say, 'They don't know how the other half live,' and I would have liked to put my thumb to my nose at them. I didn't know the exact meaning of such a gesture but I knew it was something which would upset Mother and I never did it, but it seemed a suitable action in my frame of mind.

Our back yard with steep steps down to the scullery and steep steps up to the ground floor, was bounded on three sides by other small yards. On one side a man kept pigeons which continually bleated. They didn't coo like doves in my books, but I thought they might on Winnie's wedding day. On the other side lived a retired accountant who had married his housekeeper. He had come down in the world to Poplar and spent his time, between fights with his wife, drinking heavily. His wife possessed glittering black eyes so that sometimes she had four black eyes, and the noise of her screaming when the rows were on was something terrible to hear. She seemed to goad the old man into attacking her. I thought it would make an unhappy background to a wedding to hear black-eyed Susan screaming. The funny thing was, I liked her very much, and she had two extremely beautiful and superior-looking daughters, and a delicate little son. On the third side the daughter of the house sang continually. She had a voice as good as any prima donna, reaching the highest note with ease. Even Father said it was a treat to listen to Emmy Hart so she must have possessed a remarkable voice. When I sang he would say, 'I think you must want to go to the double u,' but I still loved to sing even though he thought I had stomach ache.

Winnie calmly and gaily went on with her plans, not knowing my secret thoughts, not that it would have made any difference. Suppose the guests wanted 'to go' while the wedding breakfast was in progress. How could they step a few yards from the table to the W.C. in front of everyone? Worse still, suppose no one did, but me. This thought sent me to and from the lavatory for an hour before the wedding. Dolly always had to make sure.

Winnie's frock was made of blue silk, trimmed with lace, her hat a pretty cream straw. Marjorie was half a brides-maid as although her new frock was summery it was not so fussy that it would not do service for Sunday school on summer days. In view of my delicate condition and ap-proaching businesshood, my new frock was made of dark blue, long sleeved, and in a warm material, and it pricked. Marjorie was photographed with Winnie after the wedding on the steps of the church while the guests were throwing confetti.

Mrs Spink had been left at home while the wedding was in progress to guard the tables against marauding cats, and I wondered if she would have started on the luxurious sausage rolls and if they had been counted for one each. Although each dish was shrouded with white tissue-paper so no dust would fall on the food, I knew Marjorie and my brothers might find a way in, were they to have been left in charge. On Sundays when we were all at home Mother always counted things when she got the tea and cut the big cake ready for one piece each and so many prunes each. One day Arthur had eaten two of the stewed prunes after Mother had placed them in her china vegetable-dish on the dresser ready for 'afters.' Winnie had said, 'Now, that's not fair, Arthur, you know how Mother has to manage for us all,' and someone said, 'Pop two rabbit's eyes in the bowl, they look the same.' The numbers came out right anyway for although I knew it was only a joke I never ate my prunes because of just the thought of the rabbit's eyes. Sitting down to Sunday tea when we were all at home Agnes noticed one slice of cake short, eleven pieces instead of twelve and she began to tell a tale about a cake cut in pieces and a little girl left alone in a room with the cake. Marjorie was playing underneath the table and at this lovely story she came out to listen enthralled and when Agnes reached the part where the little girl steals a piece of cake Marjorie was beside herself with delight. 'That little girl was me,' she said proudly, and everyone laughed, well, all except me, I thought Marjorie could get away with anything.

Mrs Spink was the 'lady' who came in on washing-days to help Mother. There was a huge pile of washing and Mother would light the copper fire early on Monday morning and not finish until tea time. Mrs Spink was a very poor woman who lived in Ivy Cottages, backing on to the Grove. She was a suppressed little creature with dark hair which she did up in strips of rag to obtain a faint curl in her hair. Her husband was like a pink Humpty-Dumpty and even though he had no hair it was obvious he had been a ginger man. He worked up in the City as an export packer and I could never understand why she was so poor, for she really was. Mother said her underclothes were pitiful to see. I wondered how Mother saw Mrs Spink's underclothes for this lady always wore a long skirt, man's boots and a knitted jumper stretched out of shape with moth-holes in it. Her poverty always puzzled me for she and her husband had no children and I had often heard Mother say, 'Children keep one poor.' Mrs Spink adored my mother as though she were a creature from a different world. She insisted on calling her 'Mum' as though my mother was mistress of one of the big houses, and she thought my mother's cooking was marvellous. She got on my nerves a bit for she was always disturbing my train of thought. Mother would always have us polite, and Mrs Spink was for ever saying nonstop, 'Ain't it handsome, Dolly?' 'Ain't it grand, Dolly?' 'Ain't it beautiful, Dolly?' and Monday dinner times I spent my time saying, 'Yes, Mrs Spink, Yes Mrs Spink.' On Mondays, washing-day, when there was only Marjorie and I left at home, we always had lentil soup, cold beef with baked potatoes in their jackets into which we pushed a knob of margarine, and then a pudding. Since Mother always made Mrs Spink a cup of tea and gave her a slice of cake as well, I thought her an enormous eater for such a little person.

Once Mother gave Mrs Spink a glass of home-made ginger wine and she drove me mad, much to Mother's amusement. For weeks it was, 'Oh, the sensation, Dolly.' I supposed it was the only sensation she ever had in her life. Mother would buy mushrooms for my father and Mrs Spink would ask, 'Are them the edgecated ones, Mum?'

Father couldn't understand why Mother had to employ Mrs Spink on wash-day for had he not bought Mother the world's first washing-machine? He had brought it home proudly one day not expecting it would receive such a reception from Mother. It consisted of a broom handle at the end of which was a copper trumpet. In the trumpet where it joined the handle were circular holes and through the holes one could glimpse glass marbles. This machine had to be pumped vigorously up and down in the bath of hot soapy clothes. It needed a strong navvy to work it, or a tall Amazon. Mother treated it with disgust after Father gave the first demonstration of this wonder invention. Watched by an eager family, rolling about in hysterics, Father tottered out of the scullery wet, red, hot and exhausted and breathing heavily. The machine worked on suction and he had to keep stopping his plunging activities to tear the clothes off the trumpet. It was obvious from Mother's pursed lips that she would never use this modern invention. Father had met his match once again in Mother, and the machine was left to stand in the little L-shaped corner of the scullery where over the years it turned greener and greener. 'That's the last thing I do for your mother,' Father shouted. 'She's an obstinate woman in every respect, against progress, we *must* move with the times,' he yelled. Then he went on about the working man being his own enemy. So Mother engaged Mrs Spink.

Mrs Spink had not started on the wedding feast. The tables were a picture and everyone seemed jolly. Later we had dancing and singing, Amy recited and Winnie's young brother-in-law chased Marjorie and me all over the house, down, up, in and out until Mother called me aside and ordered me to stop. In a hoarse whisper she informed me that I musn't indulge in horse play now I had reached my teens. It was all right for Marjorie I thought, and I felt like giving her a push. Because I had been having such a good time I had forgotten all about the lavatory in the yard, in any case, Mother had said my thoughts in that direction proved to be 'mock modest.' In some way Mother had made me feel very ashamed of myself for I hadn't thought there was that mysterious dark bad thing about being chased all over the place, and I wondered if any of the guests had observed my wickedness, whatever it was, and I knew they would know all about it. I sat quietly in the front room from then on. This pleased Mother for I knew she felt I was now safe, but I began to try to describe Winnie's wedding in my thoughts with little rhymes, when into my mind came the words 'urinal union.' I stopped, horrified at my wicked brain, for Mother always gave a refined disgusted look whenever Father mentioned that he had been working down at the 'men's urinal,' and I knew that must be a filthy and vulgar establishment.

Winnie went to the Bonnington Hotel for her honeymoon. It was in London and she and her husband were to stay there until they embarked to Australia. The day she left was heartbreaking, the whole family tried to send her off happily, but it was no good. It was as though she had gone somewhere to die. The girls from Winnie's office cried too. They said they would never meet anyone else like 'Cheggie,' the office would be dead without her. As it was obvious they really meant this, Mother was very proud and she said, 'Isn't it funny how people seem to take to our family?' So we were all included in Winnie's popularity poll. I knew myself to be different from the others, I was not open and naturally 'taken to.' I knew that I was a hypocrite, a false friend, for I had to 'curry favours.'

When the vicar told us of how Judas had betrayed Jesus for thirty pieces of silver, he said the name of Judas in such terrible tones I knew that to betray for silver was the worst crime a man could commit, yet in my heart I thought Judas didn't have much choice, for it had been foretold in the scriptures. I also thought thirty pieces of silver a mighty big temptation. However, the vicar made his point and I prayed each night I would never be tempted. My friends were all convinced they would never betray a friend, but I was rather worried for myself. Of course I wouldn't betray Jesus, but a human, well, that was nearer to earth and although I agreed with my friends that we were all righteous, something inside nagged me. I knew myself better than they did.

After Winnie was gone I was swanking to my friends about the rich things Winnie had taken with her to the bush. Ivy Smith said she had been right all the time, the Chegwiddens were rich and I had told a lie when I said we weren't. Who but a rich person could buy a real tortoise-shell comb? I could see that because I was showing off my popularity was beginning to wane, and when the comb was mentioned again I repeated what my eldest sister's husband had jokingly said to Winnie, 'Real tortoise-shell, won't the fleas be stuck up.' They all laughed and at my dear Winnie's expense I regained my popularity.

I wrote to Winnie regularly, worried at her hard times. She worked like a navvy and met with disaster. Her home and possessions (oh, that real tortoise-shell comb) were destroyed by fire while she was rushing her husband to hospital on the horse-drawn waggon. Finally when it seemed prosperity was round the corner (they had a bumper wheat harvest), there was a wheat slump in Australia and I read that wheat had been dumped in the sea.

Yet Winnie, in spite of everything, found time to think of us at home. She sent me a pretty silk dress, with a portcullis arrangement round the waist. Each square of the portcullis was filled with a heavy round weight. I was so sure each weight was a silver half-crown that I unstitched the silk. But Mother was right, and Dolly shouldn't have been so unbelieving, for they *were* round discs to keep the portcullis from creasing so the frock would always look smart. I never told Winnie, but I never got it stitched back to its original chic-ness.

And, a great joy to Mother, Winnie sent Mother her first fur coat. Mother cried because she never thought she would ever have a fur coat (I didn't know she wanted one). She was touched and overjoyed with it, everyone admired it, Marjorie loved it and Mother lorded it in this fur coat at the Mothers' Union. Little cat that I was, I thought it hideous. It was, to me, an enormous coarse grassy-looking monster of a coat for it was, said Mother proudly, real kangaroo. 'And it looks it,' I said.

Mother had been the proud possessor of this kangaroo coat for some time when the General Strike took place. Father was very poorly with influenza, and as Mother was worried about Father's influenza, because he'd had pneumonia once, she placed the kangaroo coat on his bed. I thought he would turn into a gingerbread man with the weight of it for it had a heavy satin lining as well. Mother left instructions for Father not to get up at any time to go to the outside lavatory. He must use the beautiful mahogany commode which she kept in case of serious illness. It had a tapestry picture of the countryside embroidered on its lid. Father was most indignant at this invitation. His pride was so great he would have been dying before he performed on a bed-pan.

One day, during the strike, I was playing ball in the back yard when I heard the top door open very noisily and saw my father falling down the steep stone steps on a visit to the lavatory. His face was scarlet, his eyes glazed, but he had heeded Mother's warning that he must avoid a further chill. He was wearing his long pants, his best boots unlaced, the heavy furry grassy kangaroo coat, and in his delirium, realising he must keep his balding head covered, he had tied a thick woollen scarf over his head and under his chin. To crown this ensemble he was wearing three hats, a cap, a straw panama and a velour trilby, the finishing touch being a large brown paper bag, lying slightly askew the hats. They had been put away, one inside the other, in the paper bag, and they leant drunkenly on top of the scarf like the leaning tower of Pisa. He looked like an eccentric millionaire because of the fur coat.

I fell down the steps to call Mother. 'Dad's out, Dad's out,' I yelled. Mother and the rest of the family who were not out cheering the strike on, rushed into the scullery and gazed out of the windows in the scullery door waiting for the invalid's return. He staggered out of the lavatory, ensemble still intact, and was making his way to the upstairs steps when his dazed glance caught us all staring at him from down below. He tottered on the brink of the very steep steps and Mother said, 'All get back, we're hypnotising him, he'll fall down the steps and kill himself.' He gazed in a stupid way and shook his head as though in a dream, for suddenly we all disappeared from sight, but Mother's order worked like magic and he tottered up the stairs back to his sick bed and sanity. When Mother returned from tucking him in she said, 'It is true, we all have a guardian angel to look after us,' and one wag remarked that Dad's guardian angel must be rushing back to heaven to give the other angels a laugh. 'Your father is a very proud, clean living man,' said my mother.

Although lots of funny things happened during the General Strike, I think it gave me my first shadowy stirrings and feelings that there was some truth in my father's complaints about the conditions of the poor. I hated the undergraduates who came down to the East End driving vehicles. I became very afraid of the policemen having seen them beat a crowd of men round the head with truncheons. It was the first time the words 'unconditional surrender' were used, I believe, and by my father's arch-enemy, Mr Churchill. I suppose to Mr C., we were his enemy.

15 **Passing out**

A year before we left school, at fourteen, we attended on Fridays housewifery classes at Culloden Street school, the scene of my scholarship failure. The teacher was a motherly type of woman; we all knew she wasn't a real teacher, and she would train us how to be good wives, from a financial point of view, of course, to a working man. The classroom was very large, very warm, and smelt of strong carbolic soap. The tables were snow-white and I wondered why they were not worn away with all us scrubbers.

As we entered, facing us was a large blackboard on which was permanently written, 'A nourishing meal for a poor family of six.' Three fresh herrings, two lb. of potatoes, and underneath were the words, 'If a pudding is needed and able to be provided, then a suet pudding with black treacle.'

At the end of the year we were told that if we passed out as good housewives we would be given a certificate to that effect. I thought I would try hard to get this certificate for then I could show it to Mr Right, whom Mother said I would meet one day when I was really grown up. I thought I was grown up when I went to housewifery, but I knew what she meant. Everybody married a Mr Right, providing of course they met him. I asked Mother how I would know it was he, and Mother said, mysteriously, that I would recognise him when I saw him.

We were told that each day of a working housewife should have some special job in addition to everyday work. Mondays would be washing-day. So that we would be doing proper washing, we brought up soiled garments from home. Mother sent me with a little tray-cloth and a clean pair of stockings, and was horrified when I told her some of the girls brought the most filthy things and big bundles from home, so that the water seemed to become muddy and black very quickly. The washing was shared among us and I hated the thought of washing bloomers, even though they might be a friend's. Mother said her tray-cloth was dirtier than when she sent it, and she sniffed, and put it in the scullery to give it a good boil-up when she did her washing.

Before we started the washing we had to inspect all the clothes and garments, tack with big stitches round the stains so we could give them an extra scrub in the zinc baths, take all breakable buttons off, for the mangles with heavy wooden rollers would smash them to smithereens (the buttons had to be sewn on again afterwards), and sew on any missing tapes. I wondered how my mother ever had time to do any cooking on washing-day, let alone sing and play with us as she always did when I was little.

I didn't like the paragraph in the good housewives' book, where it said, 'morning work in the kitchen,' followed by another enormous list of jobs. This worried me so much I spoke to Amy about it. She said, when she was at housewifery and saw the 'afternoon work in the kitchen' paragraph, she thought she'd take no notice of that, for when she got married she wasn't going to work in the afternoons. I admired her for her bravery but secretly thought how could she do the morning work either, if there was no one to get her up in the mornings, no Mother to call her, no parrot to scream her name and make her come downstairs? If her husband had gone to work she would stay in bed all day, for when we others had gone into the country she just slept on and on at home, and the office manager sent someone down in the afternoon because he was worried, as he knew Miss Chegwidden was alone in the house, and she was still asleep when the messenger came.

The great day came when we should pass out of the housewifery class and receive our certificates. The final test before we received these happened on the last day at the school. We cooked a meal for the Culloden Street teachers. Mrs Wilson put me in charge of the mashed potatoes. Ever my favourite, I knew I would get added good remarks on my certificate because the teachers would never have tasted mashed potatoes like mine. Where Mrs Wilson went wrong, although she didn't know it at the time, was in giving me a whole packet of margarine for the potatoes. She said, 'Put on the mashed potatoes, one nut.' I already knew that, but I thought I would put about two nuts because I wanted the Culloden Street teachers' extra approval. Once I had put two nuts I couldn't stop, and over-generous, I ended up using the whole packet. I thought my potatoes looked really rich and delicious. Mrs Wilson nearly choked with temper when she saw them and the whole class had to turn to and cook more potatoes. They were annoyed with me for making them late home, Mrs Wilson looked as though she would strike me, and the teachers had to wait for their dinner, and I thought they had never seen really nice mashed potatoes before. I did not get my certificate.

On my last day at school the morning broke cold, crisp and clear, but for the first time I was loath to rise. When I came downstairs Mother and Marjorie were having breakfast, and Len, home on leave from the Navy, was sitting, reading the newspaper, by the fire. When he saw my dejected appearance he made a comical face and gave a comical sort of twitch. He couldn't bear anyone to be miserable and it was his way of trying to make me laugh, but irritably I thought, if he's not careful he'll have St Vitus's dance. Marjorie was chatting away to Mother, all about nothing, I thought; anyway what did she have to worry about? Mother said, 'Cheer up, Dolly, don't make your unhappy life miserable.' Marjorie thought this saying most comical and went into a bleating sort of laughter like a goat. This was much appreciated by Mother, but I thought it a most stupid saying and, if anything, guaranteed to make me feel more miserable than I already was. As I went out into the scullery to wash Mother and Marjorie lowered their voices, like conspirators, and I put my ear to the kitchen door to listen for I was sure they were talking about me. Len, unaware of what I was doing, pushed open the kitchen door and it cracked me on the temple. He was very upset and full of apologies but Mother said sternly, 'Listeners never hear any good of themselves.' This was true in my case but I added it to my list of 'stupid remarks,' deciding to work out later why I knew it was a silly saying.

I had been busy at school for some weeks training my successor, who, I felt, was not as reverent towards the position, or me, as she should have been, for although I hardly knew her she had jumped the barrier from subservient trainee, to a companions-in-crime attitude from the start. It was therefore difficult to teach her the job from my 'almost a mistress' position for she possessed a silent quizzical 'come off it, Dolly Chegwidden' look, and so I dropped my voice of authority and taught her from the democratic old pals' position. She really didn't need teaching, for although a sleepy-looking girl, continually yawning, her mind was as sharp as a needle. Until then I always thought people were, mentally, as I saw them physically. Her yawns hypnotised me and we traversed the school like two gold-fish, open-mouthed, gasping for water. In turn I hypnotised my family and the yawns spread. Mother was afraid I was becoming anaemic and thought she'd buy some iron tonic for me.

I always felt that in the dim future, when I too, was something in the City, I would be warmed by Marjorie's 'Oh, Dolly, Miss Wilkie does miss you, she says you were a sad loss to the school.' This was one dream shattered by the new P to be. She would be calm and worry about nothing, and I had to admit to myself she would be a perfect prefect. Still, perhaps I would get a little credit, for Miss Wilkie would have believed I had trained my successor so efficiently.

The morning dragged on. I had no official duties and I was in the classroom, for my P had already been removed from my chest, but I knew the two holes made by the safety-pin at the back of the badge would always remain on that dress for I had worn my shield of office for many, many months. For the first time we had silent reading, there was no point in lessons when we were leaving. What more could we learn in the few hours remaining? It was obvious to Mother, when I went home to dinner, that her bright saying had not dispersed the clouds for me and it was a quite dinner-time although Mother sympathetically reminded me that no one could be young for ever, we all had to grow up sometime. I didn't mind growing up, but I wanted to grow up in a school. I think I worried Mother – she may have thought my mental development had been arrested in some way. Quite out of character, she gave me $\frac{1}{2}$d. to spend, and then I knew why she had cried when she had received a postal order when I was little. Normally a gift of money would bring great joy, now when I looked at my $\frac{1}{2}$d. on the way back to school I felt like crying.

There was a strange excitement abroad, my friends were eager for the four o'clock bell to go. In a few days they would have 'wages for their mums.' Since my mother never discussed money – money was an evil word in her vocabulary – I had never longed to bring wages home to her. What money did I need for myself? Miss Cook made lovely frocks for me, out of nothing. My library books were free. I was a source of great amusement for my friends on that last afternoon.

Miss White entered the classroom carrying a basket containing brown foolscap envelopes. THE GIRL'S CHARACTER. Characters were very important, passports to livelihood to be cherished, and of course, to be kept very clean, and only to be opened by one's parents. (Lots of the girls opened them on the way home and seemed to think them very funny.) 'I have no character for you, Chegwidden,' announced Miss White, 'Miss Wilkie will give you yours if you go along to her study now.' I suddenly felt all warm, I knew Miss Wilkie was thinking of me.

The headmistress was at her desk, writing, as I entered her room and I stood respectfully at a distance until she looked up. The new prefect was just leaving the study and such a strange thought entered my mind, 'The King is dead, long live the King.' I felt like a King pronounced dead when only paralysed, watching, helplessly, a successor he didn't want, crowned.

'Well, Chegwidden,' Miss Wilkie's kind voice brought me back to reality. 'I wanted to give you your character per-

sonally and to wish you every success in the world outside.'
She handed me my character saying she would like me to
read it aloud to her. It was a truly wonderful character and
I knew it would give me a high position in life for it said I
would be a credit to any prospective employer. It ended
with the words, 'And with her warm and attractive personality, I am confident she will go far.' I was overjoyed and
could not stop my mouth from smiling. It was as good as
winning a medal. No one in the family had received a
character with these words on it, so far as I could recall.

Miss Wilkie shook hands with me, but as I turned to go,
she said, 'Oh, just a minute, Chegwidden.' For one awful
moment I thought she was going to say she had handed me
the wrong character, but she said, 'Before you go, perhaps
you would put these papers on the fire for me.' Always quick
off the mark, never waiting for people to finish their sen-
tences, I threw the papers on to the huge fire. The headmistress was a chilly mortal who always looked as though
she was shivering; her skin was always goose-pimpled, and
her study like an oven with the coke fire always half-way
up the chimney. She sat, at her desk, with her back to the
fire and so hadn't seen my efficient handling of the papers.
They flared up so quickly I thought I would catch the
chimney on fire and I took up the poker with which to hold
the papers down. The heat was so intense it almost burnt my
hand and my head felt as though it would burst.

At the noise of the poker Miss Wilkie turned round, and
let out a terrified scream. She was always so calm and dignified this unearthly scream made my heart jump. 'You sense-
less, stupid girl,' she shouted, half-choking, 'I said file, not
fire.' She fell across the room to a corner cupboard, while I
stood transfixed with fright, and brought out a thick round
piece of shiny wood in which was fixed a long sharp skewer.
She thrust this at me several times, saying between her
teeth, 'File, file, file.' Had it been a sword and I an honourable Japanese prefect I would have thrown myself on it with
remorse, or fright, so ghastly did I feel. Had she decided to
stab me with the skewer, in her fencing fashion, even though

I still held the long poker which would have been a match for her 'sword,' I would have fallen without resistance. I felt stabbing was nothing less than I deserved, for it appeared the documents were irreplaceable. 'The trouble with you, Chegwidden,' said Miss Wilkie, her face still red with annoyance, 'you *will* act and speak before you even start to think, it is your great failure, and I tremble to think how you will get on in the outside world unless you make every effort to overcome this.' So my character was a lie. Would she ask for it back? How could I go home and face them all without a character?

It was of the utmost importance to my mother that none of her girls should lose their characters, sometimes it seemed the one worry of her life. My sisters and brothers had all kept theirs. It would be just 'like Dolly' to be the first one to lose her character. At the age of fourteen too! I knew, too, that once having lost one's character, one can never get it back. Always on the look-out for escapes from tricky situations, always ready with an excuse (Mother's words), I thought if I put the character in my pocket the headmistress might not, in her present hysterical state, think about what she had written. I didn't *want* to fold it, that was bad, but it was the lesser of two evils, and, surreptitiously, I thought, I pushed it into the pocket of my frock. Lovely Miss Cook to always give me a pocket. Sadly I realised I was not the clever girl I secretly thought I was, I had no idea that a file was anything but the metal rasp my father had in his tool bag.

Miss Wilkie suddenly shook off her distress, as a dog shakes off water. She sat down at her desk, and, although holding her head, she said calmly, but wearily, 'Go now Chegwidden, and do try to curb your impetuosity.' I left, happily relieved to be gone from that room for ever – yet a few hours before I felt I should leave it regretfully in tears.

I was still hot and trembling when I passed the little sweet shop on the corner opposite the school. I had lost my desire to spend my half-penny there for the last time, in spite of the lovely selection the shop contained. Soap sugar (dirty off-white misshapen lumps of soapy acid sweetness), tiger nuts (tiny shrivelled 'dried peas' with very tough outer skins which made one cough), locust (dried, dusty, broken, sugary brown pods), chinese coconuts (round, brown, billiard balls, hard as steel, which took days of sucking before the thin brown skin came off to reveal an ivory ball which could never be eaten but only sucked, tastelessly, for ever). My father said, 'It's not confectionery, it's bloody cattle fodder they sell the kids.' But we loved it all.

I walked slowly home, deep in thought. The future was a kaleidoscope – I could not know what would evolve, or even what pattern I wanted. The past already seemed like a misty panoramic landscape, yet special happenings, happy and sad, seemed to stand out as distinct shapes – tableaux. I knew this day would be one of stark remembrance.

When I finally arrived home I told Mother nothing of my burning activity of the afternoon, although she put her hand up to my forehead and remarked I mustn't get ill now, for I had to be up early in the morning to choose a job from the *Daily Telegraph*. I handed her my character which she read silently, without emotion, until she came to the last paragraph, about my attractive personality, and then she became happy and excited. 'That is so true, Dolly, and I've always said it' (praise from Mother at last, something salvaged from the wreck of my day) 'people always take to us.' At long last I was included with the others.

I could never remember what I did with that ha'penny.

16 Something in the City

No time must be lost between school and work, and I got up early the following morning to buy the *Daily Telegraph* for Mother said the best office jobs were advertised in that expensive paper. The house was quiet and Mother left me alone in the kitchen to search through the columns of small print. No one seemed to want an office girl that Monday morning, and Mother was not surprised for Tuesdays and Thursdays were the lucky days. There was, however, an advertisement in it for trainee telephonists. 'Call at Snow Hill between ten o'clock and two o'clock,' it said. Leonard was home on leave from the Navy and Mother thought it a good idea for me to apply, as Leonard could take me there. It poured with rain while we were waiting for the bus and we arrived at Snow Hill looking like two drowned rats. I completed my application form, did a test of spelling and sums, quite simple, and so I was one of the lucky applicants to obtain the final interview.

Len insisted on coming into the interview-room with me. He had promised Mother to look after me, although I felt I was looking after him. Behind a desk sat a very severe elderly-looking woman, with black hair scraped tightly into a bun on the top of her head. She wore a lace collar round her neck, stiffened with whalebone up to her chin. Her face was yellow, long and thin, her eyes very black, and dangling on her immense bosom were gold pince-nez spectacles. I knew when she looked at us she didn't like us, and the way she said Poplar, I knew she didn't like that place either, but she said I passed my test with full marks. That's it, I thought, I'm a telephonist, won't everyone at home be proud of me. No one had reached such heights, success had come to me only a few hours after leaving school. I was miles away in my lovely dream world when the supervisor said, 'Say, round the rugged rock the ragged rascal ran.' I said it beautifully for no one could catch Dolly. I was the champion tongue twister sayer, we played tongue twisters every Christmas. Amazement and disgust on the supervisor's face. 'You have had fourteen years in which to roll your r's,' she admonished, 'and cannot do so, I'm afraid I have no vacancy for you, all my girls roll their R's.' I was on the point of tears, I hadn't expected such a thing, I was a dismal failure at the start. Len was so upset for me he said belligerently, 'She's only just fourteen, she can learn, can't she?' What could she say to this? I was to have six weeks in which to accomplish this art, and then return for a test. I sat up in the front room at home and rolled my R's all day. Father said I would drive him mad, I got a sore throat, but finally trilled like a canary. I went by myself to Snow Hill at the end of six weeks, but all vacancies had been filled.

I was an unemployed failure, a drain on my family. I decided I would walk part of the way home to save Mother some money, and I passed a large building in a turning near Ludgate Circus, outside which stretched a long queue of girls. I joined on the queue and waited hours, for the queue stopped moving when the interviewer went to lunch. Then I was on top of the world again, out of those many, many girls I had won the job. 'That's because of your lovely smile,' said Mother.

It was a boring office, the staff played practical jokes on each other all day long, at least when Captain Nicholson wasn't there. He was the owner, an irritable-looking man, tall, thin, with a military moustache. My desk was by the glass entrance doors and I would glance up sometimes when people entered. One morning, I had been there about a week, Captain Nicholson stopped at my desk instead of sweeping through without looking at anyone. Everyone looked over surreptitiously, Capt. Nicholson never spoke to the staff. I gave him a bright smile, I knew he was going to praise me for my work. He put his face close to mine and hissed, 'If I see you smile again, I shall pay you orff.' I was so frightened I laughed hysterically into his face and was despatched with my cards, and sent home in tears. Father said, 'Don't let that miserable old bugger upset you, gel, I know what some of them are like. I've had to nurse a lot of them and show them what to do,' and he gave such a comical imitation of some of the officers he had 'nursed' that Mother and I were soon laughing. 'Cheer up,' said Mother. 'Don't make your unhappy life miserable, you'll soon get a job.'

I got a job the following week with wholesale grocers in Spitalfields. I was happy as a sandboy there. The warehouse men, like twins, in brown overalls and grey caps, Bert and Fred, would plunge the cheese-tasters into a big cheese and give me a long stick to have with crusty bread and huge lumps of butter from their slabs. I answered the phone, stamped the letters, learnt to type with two fingers, and was the office pet. Work was lovely. The office manager was a dear old man. One day he asked me when my birthday was. I said it was that very day and he gave me a huge box of chocolates tied with a big red ribbon. I had stupidly been joking, I never thought anyone would give me a birthday present. I told him of my dishonesty and he allowed me to keep the chocolates on the understanding I realised that in life honesty was the best policy. It didn't sound quite right to me in view of the fact that I was allowed to keep the chocolates. Mother was proud that I was thought of so highly. But all good things come to an end, I knew that by now, and into the office came another office manager, a Mr Wilson, an old sergeant-major type with no sense of humour in the whole of his Gallipoli bosom. He ousted the kind office manager, and brought his niece in 'to help me.' Since I had so little to do I should have seen the red light. His niece was a jolly girl and we had great fun together. One day we were being merry when Mr Wilson said if I had nothing to do I should take myself off to the warehouse and clean out 'the desk.' This desk had been the lying-in home for all the warehouse cats from time immemorial and I cheekily said I was not employed as a warehouse-cleaner. Instant dismissal and sad arrival at no. 13 Grove Villas. It was amazing how my father was always on my side in these crises. 'Bloated capitalists,' he yelled. 'Write for a week's money, it's your entitlement.' I wrote and received a letter to the effect that if I desired another week's money (12s. 6d.) I must do another week's work.

My next job lasted one day. It was very strange and I never knew what it was all about. It was in an office above a shop on Ludgate Hill. I was told to sit in a tiny office, without a window and look at some old magazines while the man who engaged me went into an inner office with a woman of about thirty. I sat there all day and got fed up looking at these old magazines, all about engines, then the man came out, gave me three shillings and said my services were no longer required. Again I made a written request for one week's money. This time the letter was returned marked 'Not known at this address.' Mother seemed to think I had had a lucky escape from some dark mysterious terror.

She was getting worried about me now. My career was, to say the least of it, erratic and she asked Amy, who worked for a local engineer if she would speak for Dolly, which Amy did, and Mother helped me get ready for the interview. She wanted me to be specially presentable for she wanted Amy to be proud of me. She had bought me a beige woollen jumper suit through a friend who obtained it at wholesale price. Mother thought it looked both good and ladylike and the colour suited me well. I had a little beige hat from the 'jumble,' beige gloves, beige stockings and beige shoes. Father said I could 'take the biscuit' and laughed. Mother called me back when I reached the front gate and said, 'Wait a minute' and ran upstairs. She came down with a look of delight on her face and I thought she was the most unselfish person in the world. One of my sailor brothers had brought her home a pale lavender scarf, hand-painted with orchids in purple, white and yellow. It was known as Mother's scarf and kept in tissue-paper in a little box in the small drawer of the mahogany chest-of-drawers. It smelt of lavender as she placed it round my neck and I felt very proud and honoured and said I wouldn't even crease it. Mother said it 'made' the outfit, and off I went followed by the admiring glances of Mother, Father and Marjorie.

As I went past the library I wished I had been getting a book out for I could have surprised the assistant into thinking I was a lady. Finally I reached Pennyfields, the Chinese quarter. I thought I would make a detour. For one thing I might be taken for the white slave traffic in my best clothes, and for another, I was always afraid a Tong war would break out. I had a friend who lived in Oriental Street which was next to Pennyfields and she remembered the Tong wars. They weren't allowed out to play while the war was on but they looked out of their front room behind the lace curtains to see all the little Chinese men running along with their wounded. They wheeled these men on covered hand carts. The carts looked like Chinese dhows on wheels. But the Chinese only fought each other. They had puckapoo shops and lots of people who lived near there bought a puckapoo sheet each week. It had Chinese lettering on it so I thought they were clever to know when they had won. My mother thought it was terrible to gamble at puckapoo.

Charlie Brown's was near Pennyfields. It was a big public house and he had a lot of unusual curios the foreign seamen sold him. My friend said Charlie Brown had a pickled baby in a jar. He was her landlord and he came to collect the rents on a white horse. She said he was a lovely landlord and if he knew it was a child's birthday he would give the child 6d. from the rent. She said when it was her birthday her mother would give her a nudge when she was paying the rent to remind her so she would get her sixpence. I wished we'd had Charlie Brown for a landlord, just to see his white horse, but I knew I wouldn't get sixpence, my mother would never nudge me. Why she wouldn't even have let me go to the door on my birthday if Charlie Brown was our landlord. Mother was so funny not wanting people to give us things I thought.

Finally I arrived at the Lion Packing Factory and rang the bell in the little waiting-room, for it said on it, 'Please ring.' A spotty young man with a pencil behind his ear came in and when I said I was Miss Chegwidden and I'd come for an interview, he blushed and said, 'Follow me, please.' I followed him into a large office where there were a lot of spotty young men sitting at a counter on high stools. They all had pencils behind their ears, and they all looked at me trying not to let me know they were looking. As I passed a thick green curtain, I was startled out of my interview feeling, for Amy's head popped out and she hissed, 'You've got Mother's scarf on.' I felt awful that she had accused me, in front of all these strangers, of taking Mother's scarf without permission. She must have known it was a thing I would never do, and I started to tell her how I came to be wearing it, but she said, 'Go on, don't stand gossiping here, Mr Bartlett's waiting for you.' I was so upset by Amy's accusation and by her informing the office I was wearing borrowed finery, that I don't think I answered up very brightly at my interview, but I got the job, I suppose really because Amy was a wizard with figures.

I worked for a Mr Ablett. Acid tablet the boys called him. He was very kind to me, but he and Amy disliked one another. She thought he was always gazing at my legs and he was disdainful of Amy, because although she had a fiancé, the rich Swiss in charge of the foreign office was head over heels in love with Amy, and showed his feelings not only to Amy but to the world. Mr Ablett, a religious man, thought Amy was playing fast and loose. I tried to leap on to the stool like the young men did. I thought in this way I could hold my skirts down and not expose my legs, but I overshot the stool and had to be assisted from the floor to a chair and smoothed down by Mr Ablett.

I went to Buzzards in Oxford Street and purchased hand-made chocolates for Mr Ablett to put in the Christmas boxes the firm sent to customers, and he gave me a diamond-shaped velvet bag with home-made chocolates in it because I had got everything correctly. I would have been happy for life there and would have done well, I feel, but the firm moved to Surrey, and it was back to the City again as there wasn't much locally in the way of vacancies for office girls.

17 Impending doom

At seventeen, as Mother considered me to be now a young lady, I was allowed to put my hair up. I would have liked to have had it bobbed, but daren't mention such a criminal act to my parents, for they had never got over the shock of Amy's brazenness when she had arrived home one day minus her lovely long, thick, dark tresses. She pranced into the kitchen thinking she looked truly beautiful. I thought she did, but Mother, shocked to the core, said in a great temper, 'Get out of my sight, away from me, for you look just like a little monkey.' Father, always alert to the rights of the individual, even though it never got him anywhere, despatched one of the boys to the barber's for the return of Amy's shorn locks. I thought he intended to use them in his plumbing work, mixing them with tallow, even though the coil of waxed hair he used in his work was yellowish and snuff-coloured.

The barber, a Jewish man, called, strangely, Jesus, refused to part with Amy's hair and my father got in a swearing temper. I thought his remarks about Jesus not at all religious. Dad was certain that some blue-blooded duchess or, even worse, the rich wife of a bloated capitalist would be lording it about in a wig made of Amy's rich dark hair, and she the daughter of a red-hot socialist. I got the impression from my father that all aristocratic men were disease-ridden and all possessed bald-headed wives because of the rich food and wine they consumed, and I was so glad my favourite meal was sausages and I knew I would hate wine. No, it was much better to be poor – healthier according to Father – holier according to the vicar and so much easier to enter the kingdom of heaven – even though putting up my abnormally thick and unruly hair was proving a difficult task for Mother and a miserable time for me.

Mother had to agree it did not suit me in a bun on the top of my head. Someone remarked at that stage that it looked as though a swarm of birds or bees would fly out of my crown if a gun had been fired. In the end, my hair was divided into two thick uneven plaits. I wore a plaited circle over each ear called earphones. Ever after I lived in a quieter, more muffled world. As I almost had to lip-read and gazed intently at people while they were speaking to me, I gained the fine reputation of being a most sympathetic listener, and because of my direct staring look, a sincerely honest girl.

To keep my unruly earphones from falling down I was forced to use packets of iron hair-pins and my ears became almost permanently doubled over as ledges for my plaited coils. Coinciding with the raising of my tresses I suffered other distresses, I suddenly became acutely self-conscious, and shy. I went through an agonising period of daily stage fright. Walking in the city streets to and from work and at lunchtime was sheer torture. I would wonder if I could walk across the pavement and reach the kerb with normal strides, or if I would be forced to take a couple of small mincing steps to get me down or up the kerbs safely. Would my normal paces take me beyond the kerb making me fall, or would I have to execute a shuffled hesitation at the kerb, and so cause a pile up of stockbrokers and city gents and ladies walking quickly behind me, unaware of impending doom? I would be underneath, unable to make a quick getaway.

In addition to this very real fear, if that wasn't enough, I was sure that my bloomers would fall down one day in the City. Suppose they fell down just as I was negotiating a kerb, how could I emerge from beneath the pile-up minus my bloomers, although perhaps if there were other ladies in the pile-up I could say they weren't mine? I took to wearing packets of safety-pins round the whole of my waist, pinning to my vest and petticoat the offending garment which was so set, I was sure, on doing an Isaac Newton on me. When I undressed at night and piled up the piles of hair- and safety-pins, Marjorie said I could have opened an ironmonger's shop. Mother laughed at me and said I must avoid shops which sold magnets, or I might be dragged inside. When she saw my worried face she said, well, perhaps only pinned to the window.

My seventeenth year was a fearful one for me, small wonder that reaching the haven of my home, I stayed there, finding a more relaxed world of satisfaction in my books, and the green apples which I consumed non-stop. The doctor must have been wrong when he had insisted I was a gastric child, for I loved green apples, and they caused me no discomfort.

The job I had at General Buildings, Aldwych, was just up my street. The work was simple, the office staff easy-going, the wages enough for my needs and I settled down happily sure that an easy-going Mr Right was just around the corner. Mother would be pleased and life would go on without problems or calamities. At this firm was a young man, of good background, who came from Surrey. There was nothing between us, he was younger than me, he came to me for advice, and from my eighteen-year-old maternal and older-woman position I advised on life's problems and encouraged him in his ambitions to get on. Someone had given him an old motor-bike and he would tell me of his prowess on this wonderful and modern machine. As Mother believed me when I exaggerated as to my progress, so in a motherly way I believed this young man, and when one evening he suggested he drove me home to Poplar, I agreed, for I was saving up for a winter coat, and to save the sixpenny fare was a great incentive.

I waited in the Aldwych for this young man to appear and hardly recognised him for he was dressed as for a trip to the moon with an airman's flapped cap, enormous dark goggles, a mask, a thick fleecy-lined leather coat, wading leggings and laced boots. This ensemble convinced me he was the expert he had always vowed he was.

I sat on the pillion, finding it difficult to balance myself, and had to stretch painfully to get my arms around him. If I had not been afraid of hurting this young man's feelings I think I would have changed my mind about saving my fare at that moment. I was embarrassed, too, that my skirt had gone up to show more of my calves than was decent. However after the driver bashed the pedal down several times with no result and I was wobbling dangerously, suddenly with a terrific roar we shot off and I felt we were heading for the inside of the law courts. In a flash I knew this young man was not the efficient dirt-track rider he had boasted to me he was. I was panic-stricken and in pain for scalding hot splashes of water were spurting over the inside of one of my legs. Terrified I would fall off the back of the pillion and be run over, I tugged at my chauffeur with all my strength, anxious not to be the girl he left behind. He was mouthing something I couldn't decipher (I learnt later he, too, was terrified at being pulled off the bike, my hold was so limpet-like), and we reached Aldgate in no time, swaying perilously all the time. We went round the wrong side of a tram in Commercial Road, the tram-driver swore at us and people on the pavements stopped and stared in amazement. I was sure I would not see my family again and was sorry for the unkind things I had done and said to them all my life. They were all so lovely in my final memories of them. Fortunately the young man was efficient at turning the bike and we arrived in Arthur Street. Shaking, dirty, bits of grit in my eyes, my hair had come down, my leg was red and wet, I tottered up the Grove, thankful Mother hadn't seen me, unaware that news had already spread like wildfire before me. 'Your Dolly's in Arthur Street with a big man on a motor-bike.'

I entered the peace and calm of no. 13. Mother was sitting in a chair with her Judge Jeffreys face on. She usually jumped up on my arrival, but this time she sat silently still. Marjorie, and Agnes who was visiting and waiting for her husband, and Amy and her fiancé stood by, a silent jury. No one smiled or said hallo, and I stammered out, 'What's the matter?' 'Matter?' said Mother. 'You have something to tell me.' 'No,' I said, looking every inch a criminal. 'What do you mean?' 'Well,' said Mother in a tone of great triumph, 'you were seen with a man getting off a motor-bike in Arthur Street.' She said Arthur Street as though it were

Sodom and Gomorrah. I glared at Marjorie, obviously the spy responsible for my presence in the dock. Marjorie promptly burst into tears. Mother was now angry that innocent little Marjorie should be accused and Mother didn't want the subject turned by attention being paid to Marjorie. Agnes started to cry in sympathy with her sister. I thought Mother enjoyed her judge's role in a way, for she was sure right was on her side. The difficulty was that I was not sure what crime I was charged with, and it would have been impossible to ask, for that would make Mother more cross than ever. I saw my Ethel Mannin book opened on the dresser. Oh, God, surely Mother hasn't been reading that. Ethel Mannin was so modern and before our time. I knew what page the book was open at. 'She came willingly to his arms and it seemed to them both that two dark rivers had mysteriously flowed together, first on a high flood in spate and then reaching the calm flowing of one river now,' or something to that effect. Perhaps Mother knew what it meant. I didn't.

I tried to say I had just had a lift home with the office boy, but I caught sight of myself in the mirror, I looked as though I'd been dragged home through the jungle. In tears, rage, and pain I ran out of the room and up to bed. I knew I should have thought before riding on a motor-bike. No one did that, only 'fast' girls. Mother knew I was not fast, so why did she always worry so about me?

18 **Odd jobs**

All I ever wanted was a peaceful existence, and no one seemed to want to leave me alone. Arthur's wife had heard of a vacancy for a shorthand typist with a firm of rating surveyors and valuers in Bridewell Street. The wages were 35s. per week which was more than many men were getting then. Now my chickens were coming home to roost for I had boasted of my shorthand speeds. All lies. I couldn't tell Mother I was a liar, that would be the last straw. I couldn't refuse the interview, the family would not have allowed it. Perhaps, I hoped, I wouldn't get the job. But I did.

I was in an office with three of the most expert stenographers I ever met in the whole of my City life. They were elderly but rapid workers. I had one week's reprieve from execution for the boss was away rating public houses in Hampshire, and I did some copy-typing and got to know 'les girls.' They were very motherly to me and very kind. I should have told them my dread secret, but I hoped something would happen to me before it was discovered. I hadn't had appendicitis, I prayed for that. My prayers remained unanswered, and a week after I started at Bridewell Street I was summoned to the boss's office. I had been warned he was the fastest dictator in the city. They said he started dictating as he heard the office door open.

This doom-laden morning he had filled the other girls' notebooks full and the number five sign in the glass box on the wall, waggled. Up I got, new notebook, sharpened pencil. They were right. As I opened the door I heard a voice talking at great speed about hereditaments in Dorset. I wrote down 'h' perhaps I'd remember some of it. My pencil broke and as I reached the typist's chair my tears fell fast and sudden. Gone was the great dictator. As I poured out my sobbing story he began to laugh. He passed me a clean white handkerchief and said he would pay for me to attend the city of London College in Ropemaker Street until I was proficient in shorthand. In the meantime I could take slow dictation from the many young men articled to his firm. He said I was a young lady of promise. I didn't know what he meant, but he said the young men would be pleased to help me. And they were. All sorts and sizes of young men came to that office, all very upper class, and all charming, and each one helped me with dictation. It was, I thought, quite pleasurable. But in the outer office was a very ancient lady filing-clerk. Her minion was a tiny cockney office-boy, delicate, anaemic, with enormous bags under his eyes. I often used to think these bags were the largest thing about him.

I was coming through the outer office one day, the first one back from lunch, the office deserted and quiet, when this young boy flung himself at me and smothered me with kisses. He was like a limpet, I just couldn't tear him off. I was furious. If someone came into the office what would they think of me? I was the older one, I would have led him astray. No one, I guaranteed, would have believed that a boy of this office-boy's age would have such feeling. I thought there must be something radically wrong with him, he certainly wasn't a boy. I dragged myself away, I daren't tell anyone, who would believe me, and I didn't want him to get the sack because he needed the money. I warned him what I would do if he ever did such a wicked thing again, and he just grinned and smacked his lips. So every lunch-time I either had to be late back from lunch, or wait until the elderly lady returned to the outer office from wherever she was wont to disappear. I could have coped with any of the charming young men, but this brazen boy, delighted with his prowess, was like a mosquito on the back of a rhinoceros.

I knew I could never take to my home any of the young men articled there, but the matrimonial committee of elderly ladies didn't, and neither did the young men. I went to the theatre with one young man and to Scottish dancing with another who had delightful brothers and a charming father, but his mother, straight-faced and unbending insisted on addressing me as Miss Chegwidden, plied me with questions as to what my father did, why I lived in Poplar, and what my brothers and sisters were. When she knew I had nine, she nearly collapsed. I wanted to tell her not to be frightened for her son, but who could blame her?

Each year the senior partner took us all to lunch in a Surrey hotel, then home to his large house at Esher where we played games, won prizes, and had tea. He had a beautiful garden with a small river running through it. He was a charming man but he never took off his bowler-hat and when he passed me a large gun for target shooting – everybody had to try everything – I got nervous and fired it before I should have done and one of the pellets hit his hat. He wasn't cross, in fact he showed no emotion whatsoever, he just took the gun away and passed it to the next guest. But the next year he must have remembered for when it was shooting time he waggled his finger after me and pointed to the clock golf course. His son looked after me and said I was like a cornflower in a field of thistles. I suppose I was the only young female there, and I had no competition. I could never relax as the others did. When the lady of the house asked how my garden at home was looking, balancing my delicate china cup, saucer and plate on one knee took all my attention, I didn't exactly tell a lie when I said, 'The grass needs cutting,' for we did have a couple of blades. The daughter of the house usually draped herself on the lawn. I couldn't take my eyes off her, she was like a picture from the *Queen*. She went to the Slade school of art and I felt like a clumsy red beetroot beside her.

Although the family agreed with Mother that I was no constant nymph, I was becoming irresponsible, flitting from job to job, the sure way to unemployment and ruin, Mother said. They all grudgingly agreed that at each fresh situation I was bettering myself, but although they were pleased I was still permanently employed, they felt I was tempting providence. When I began to work for the London Transport at Chiswick, they thought at last I was employed for life, a national company, no hanky-panky in the offices there, a safe and secure future, with a pension.

I would impress the family with the schedules I typed 'two yards wide,' with only just enough space for the headings. And I had a train pass, I was an executive. The family were grudgingly proud of me. The typing-pool was small, the 'head girl,' a lovely middle-aged spinster who looked like a typical mum, human and jolly, living only for her cat and her dog. She had lost all her life's savings when a private bank crashed, but she never became embittered about it, and she had such a sense of humour. We all loved her. I worked for a Mr Cook, a dear old man. He was very worried I would be unable to transcribe my shorthand (how did he guess?) and he dictated so slowly and loudly and distinctly that I used to take it all down in longhand. The embarrassing part of his dictation was the way he would spell words out, for engines have names of the most intimate parts of the male and female of the species and Mr Cook dictated to me on a dais in front of his male staff, sixty young jolly men. Their glances as I went through their office and approached the dais were the forerunner of the wolf whistle, and then when Mr Cook spelt nipple or cock, etc., I was scared to look up. He was a pure-minded man and the young men were not.

The superintendent was a fine tall man with the physique and face of the most handsome of film stars. One day I was called upon to take notes on the hearing of a serious fire and when I entered the room it was full of garage men, engineers and fire experts. I was told all their names, but when the case began, all became oblivion for I couldn't think which one was which according to the code names I had written in my book. After the case was over when Mr Williams said he would like ten copies, I did my weeping act again. He was so sympathetic and upset for me he sent for the chief engineer, who stayed with me all day and helped me sort the case out. Who got blamed for the fire I never knew!

I had Mother persuade Marjorie to accompany me to the office dance, as we could take a friend and I was rigged out in an old dress Winnie had left behind. It was white, but my underclothes were coloured. Mother said it would not be noticed in the dim lights such affairs were wont to have. The Superintendent always opened the dancing with an important member of the female staff, and to the pride and joy of Marjorie, the amazement of the whole of the London Transport staff, to my utter horror because of my coloured petticoat and because the first dance was always the superintendent solo, he came the whole length of the hall to bow like a courtier in front of me. Marjorie impressed Mother with my popularity at the London Transport and Mother said, 'Fancy,' in such puzzled tones, but I understood, I was just as puzzled by it all as she was.

19 No constant nymph

When I was twenty-one, Mother was either worried that I would become an old maid, or my constant consuming of green apples had driven her out of her mind, for she began to coax me to lead a more active social life. How to begin? I'd never had a boy friend, never been kissed, except by the baggy-eyed young man, and that wasn't kissing. Marjorie began my coming-out by taking me to a party. Here I sat in the corner, not even being called upon with a letter in Postman's Knock, one of the girls received a parcel. In the opposite corner was a young man who was the nearest thing to a frog I had ever seen, it would have needed more than a princess's kiss to change him, I thought. In a game of forfeits he came to me and paid his forfeit with a kiss. I had come out. He saw me home, and it was obvious to me I would do no better at my great age. I arranged to meet him the following week-end. Mother was pleased, for the young man had been to grammar school and his parents owned a flourishing business. When my brothers said the whole family were frogs, Mother chided them and said that a person's character was the important thing not his looks. I agreed with her, but when my father burst out laughing, having heard of my conquest, I knew I'd rather be an old maid, and I cancelled my date with the prince in disguise.

Marjorie taught me to dance. She was so expert, and we went to the Town Hall dances, Mother saying we would not meet Mr Right there. The dancing was superb. These white, poker-faced young men with their creased suits which smelt of moth-balls and tom-cats, would nod their heads. 'Coming rahnd?' and off we'd go, always being left in the middle of the floor when the dance was finished. But they could dance and so I became an expert and my quick-step was the quick-step of champions. I even used to 'feather.'

I did meet one young man different from the rest, at the Town Hall. All the girls were crazy about him and it seemed strange to me that I should be his chosen champion, for it was obvious he was serious. I knew Mother would be pleased, for he worked as a draughtsman for a national company, and there was no doubt he was on the way up. He'd even been to the Nautical and Engineering College. Coupled with all this prospective affluence he looked like Cary Grant. He even dressed like him. His suit hadn't been taken out of pawn for the Saturday night hops, it was obvious. His family must be posh, I thought, and one Saturday afternoon I was invited to tea. Well I thought that was what it was, when he arranged to meet me. His name was George. We spoke about food on the way to his house. I was a little perturbed when he said his favourite dinner was 'ash,' but hoped I'd misheard.

We arrived at a street of dingy terraced houses. It was a hot day, the front doors were open and overalled women, with rags curling their hair, were sitting on wooden chairs outside their houses. Men with silk white knitted scarves and caps were leaning in groups against the walls. No one ever sat outside in the Grove. We walked through this arch of honour of staring eyes and comments 'That's Georgy . . .'s young lady,' to the open door of his house. Along the length of the torn varnished walls of the passage hung a string of washing, men's pants, shirts, enormous women's bloomers. The house had a smell of piddled prams, and steaming copper water. We went into a little kitchen, where, by the side of a kitchen range sat a red-faced sweaty-looking woman with straw-coloured hair. Her shoes were cut so that her bunions could poke out. She neither looked at me nor spoke. Through the window I saw a gingery fat man in a collarless shirt, with dangling braces talking to some pigeons. George went out, looked at the ginger man, but neither spoke. The table was littered with dirty cups and plates and a fly was walking round the top of the milk jug. There was no little muslin cover with blue beads on such as graced our milk jug. George said, 'We are going to the pictures.' Pictures on a Sunday! My mother would faint right away if she knew, but

I was relieved to get out of the house. Would that woman come to life when I was gone? I wondered.

We went to the Grand and as we sat down George passed me a damp, stiff paper bag and said, 'These are for you,' and I felt sorry at my dreadful thoughts about his mum. Then he passed me a pin asking me not to drop it for it was his sister's best one. It was a long pin with a glass knob. I couldn't think what I wanted a pin for, and I put my hand into the bag. Boiled sweets I thought. I hated boiled sweets and I began to feel bad tempered. Whatever was in the bag gave off a horrible smell, a horrible feeling. It was dark in the pictures. What were these damp warm things? Then when I felt the little indented circles, I knew. Winkles! Ugh! and George had given them to me as though they were the greatest treat a man can give to his heart's desire. How could anyone eat winkles in the pictures? The empties would get muddled up with the full ones. What about getting the eyes off, and suppose one were bad? The whole family complained if I ever ate winkles at tea-time. I sniffed each one so many times, I was never sure when a winkle was really good and pure; they said I put them off their tea. I passed the fishy present back to George, with his sister's pin. Sadly I knew he was not Mr Right.

I flung myself into a social round to forget, and worried the life out of Mother with a different boy-friend every month or so, but it was difficult to find one who didn't have defects at least as major as mine.

Marjorie worked in the City for a firm of wholesale drapers who employed young men trainees. These young men lived in a big house at Southwark and the firm had a beautiful sports club at Eltham, where we went every Saturday for the dances and had a fine time. Still no Mr Right, until one evening I wore the first dress I ever made. The material was of figured georgette, very startling, but I had trouble with the neck. Mother thought it a bit too daring, especially when I bought emerald green shoes to go with the frock, which was flame colour. Mother said no nice young man would dance with a girl in a frock with a neck like that.

But I left the house with a scarf round my neck. This pleased Mother for she never thought I would be so daring as to take the scarf off. I did remove it and Mother was right, all the young men stayed away from me!

It was almost time to start for home when *he* arrived. My John. He was much older than the others at the firm. He was in a position of trust and lived in a flat at the top of the building overlooking St Paul's cathedral. Perhaps I was as much in love with the City as with John, or more so; and I was quite green in the ways of the world. I would go to his flat at weekends. I could choose what I liked to eat from the resident chef, John read to me, played lovely records, we saw plays, we lay on the settee, looked out at St Paul's and I thought, this is it at last, everything has come right in the end. I took him home to meet my parents, he called my father Sir, everyone liked him, I had done well; here was a man of the world, intelligent and intellectual. But Mother looked strange whenever his name was mentioned, and she began to offer to tell my fortune with the cards. I always wanted her to do this, and she usually did it grudgingly. She had never actually *offered* to do so before. She told my fortune many times in the ensuing months, and each time she pointed to the King of Clubs and said, 'I can't put my finger on it, but there is a man in your cards, not quite nice.' Then she would look at the card again and say, 'I feel he is a married man and is enticing a single girl,' but I thought it was a warning of what lay in the future.

One Saturday night I told John what my mother saw in the cards, thinking he would say, 'When we are married, I must take care and not let any nasty men come near you,' but he said, 'Your mother is right, I am married.' Then I thought, there will be no Mr Right in my life ever, and I felt very cold. He was separated from his wife, he said. I thought well, I could get over that and when he was divorced I could still marry him, no one need know but he had two sweet little girls and I couldn't take him from them. He said he had been a cad, but he couldn't help himself, that I would never know what it had cost him in terms of self-control. He could be nothing but honourable to someone like me. I thought he was being a bit novelettish and that talk of self-control was stupid. He tried to match me up with his young brother, a very clever young man, who made me laugh a lot, but he wasn't even a shadow of John. Some years later I heard that John had died of tuberculosis and I cried for the little girls.

Suddenly Marjorie and I were at a loose end at week-ends, Saturdays we went dancing, still just for dancing's sake, and on Sundays now we would go to church. After church we would walk from Blackwall Tunnel to Upper North Street, backwards and forwards until it was time to go home. All the young people did it. During my walks I had noticed a slim elegant young man, always talking seriously to his companion, who seemed to be a silent listener. I began to watch for this young man and learnt that he went to the Wesleyan Chapel, which was termed Lax's place, for the pastor was the Lloyd George of the religious world, quite famous.

I would feel my heart thump when this young man approached lecturing his friend, but I knew he had no idea I was watching out for him every Sunday. I knew when he was approaching for he was slightly bandy, attractively so I thought, and if he walked on the pavement side and I did likewise, through the crowds of promenaders I could see his slightly bent leg sticking out. It was no good, he never did notice me, this elegant young man who wore such beautiful suits. He was always miles away and in any case he didn't look the sort of young man who would speak to a girl he didn't know, and I gave up the chase.

The chapel girls arranged for Marjorie and me to spend a holiday near Sheerness in a lovely house owned by the Chapel. It was a holiday home for young people on the sea front and it cost very little to go there. Sister Annie thought we had deserted the Church and gave us a ticking off. But we still went on the holiday. We met two young men on the sea front and some months later I became engaged to one of them. His parents lived in Yorkshire, he was about to leave the R.A.F. and one week-end he arranged for us to visit them in the country. He bought me a large basket filled with

English peaches, for the journey. I offered him a peach but he refused and so – peaches always do something to me – I ate them all. As I was finishing the last one he said he would have a peach after all. I felt the greedy pig I was and although he said he was glad I enjoyed them, I thought he looked a bit shaken.

His parents were charming people; his father worked on the local newspaper. They had a lovely house, and his mother fed me on roast turkey (it wasn't Christmas), and beautiful trifles and pastries. I think I was in love with the thought of being an engaged girl and the exotic food, more than I was with him, but he was quite good looking. He was an engineer by profession, and although not very vital or lively, I thought I should have a calm life with him. The next day he took me to see his grandmother. She was wearing a sari and had a little jewel fixed in her nose. I was surprised, to say the least of it. He was blond although he had dark brown eyes, and his sister's children were blond too. I would have to tell Mother because there were such things as throwbacks and I didn't want to be different from the rest of the family. His mother gave a party for our engagement and everyone was happy for Thomas. He was a champion shot and thought a lot of a little silver gun he had.

As the weeks went on I began to feel depressed about getting married and began to be bored with my Thomas, and I wrote him that I thought I had been too hasty, with regrets I returned his ring. My brother Arthur thought I was playing too fast and loose with men's affections (Thomas was in the middle of a job on Arthur's house at Beckenham), but I didn't care. Thomas wrote and said if he couldn't have me no one else should. This worried me when I thought about the little silver pistol, but I thought it was nonsense. He lived in Yorkshire, I would never see him again.

At that time I was working for the London Orphan School and coming out into Eldon Street one lunch-time, there was Thomas, with his hand suspiciously in the pocket of his coat. Bravely I ignored him and swept on. I knew he was following me and I thought of all the people passing to and fro – they did not know that tragedy was stalking so near. I was afraid to turn back and plead with him; he might shoot me in my bosom, I'd rather be shot in the back I decided. I crossed the road to the A.B.C. and as I entered the restaurant, I decided I must live and I threw myself flat on the floor of the tea shop just as a waitress was placing a plate of poached eggs in front of an elderly woman. She looked surprised to see me prostrate and looking at me but speaking to the customer she said, 'Are you the lightly done one?' and because suddenly I was so delighted to be alive, I started to laugh at the waitress's air of tired irritability and the elderly spinsterish woman, 'the lightly done one.' I think it was assumed I was lying on the floor because I had caught my foot in the mat. I glanced out of the door and saw my avenger jumping on to a no. 11 bus. No. 11 was always my lucky number.

With the breaking of my engagement and the disapproval of all and sundry, except my parents, I was free to circulate again. I had been a bit disappointed that Thomas had not said I could keep my engagement ring as a memento when I returned it to him, but it convinced me that he had not truly loved me. Thus I eased my conscience.

I went to parties with Marjorie. The craze then was for all-night parties, much to Mother's disgust, but she had such faith in Marjorie that she thought so long as she was with Dolly this worrisome daughter would be safe. I went out with so many young men from then on that I worried no more about being on the shelf. There was a jewellery salesman in a pearl grey homburg hat and grey spats, a Humphrey Bogart sort of chappie, not my type at all, possibly that was why he fell for me. I had one setback to my pride. We had been to an all-night party, there were no such things as orgies, then, of course. We just played games and when we became tired, the lights would be put out and we cuddled up in a chair or some nook with the young man of our choice. We only ever kissed, but it was very enjoyable and when dawn broke we would have breakfast and arrive home to sleep until the afternoon.

At one party one young man asked to speak to me in the

garden for a moment. I went eagerly, I was in demand these days, I thought. He said it was his one desire in life to possess me, and in a round about way I thought he was making an appointment that very night to be the bailiff. In a firm and dignified manner I told him he was a disgusting person, he must know I was not that sort of girl. He then said he only offered me a night's delight, and I should think it over carefully, as he knew it was the only chance I would ever have of such an offer. I knew he meant for himself and all mankind. I was speechless at the insult but secretly worried in case it was true and I couldn't see myself as others saw me. I thought, it would be better to be a Nun with no worries, just to live in a lovely garden and think beautiful thoughts, and never meet up with proposals that were not very nice. And they could walk along the road without disgrace if their drawers fell down, for their voluminous skirts would hide their accidents.

Then I met John the second. He was such a gentle creature, as safe as houses my mother would have said. We would walk to Blackwall Pier in the dusk of evening and sit on a seat overlooking the lovely river and he would hold my hand, kiss me, and be in another world. His eyes would be closed and he was gone. He was no bother at all and it was very pleasant. His kiss was really sweeter than wine, and I could, while this was in progress, gaze out at the lights on the river, listen to the lap-lap of the water and the barges nudging against each other. The moon would rise and light up the water with silver, John was in his heaven, and I could think about all sorts of other things. If I'd had a book full of dictation from a boss that evening I would get all the difficult parts clear in my mind, I planned my next outfit, and so on.

I would have been sitting on the pier for ever if Marjorie hadn't discovered a tennis club we could join, although at that time we had barely hit a ball with a racquet. It was in the playground of a school at Plaistow, and we were moving up in the world now. We bought tennis frocks and hold-alls and left for the club every Saturday after lunch. The club-house was the infants' cloakroom and the two courts were bumpy and uneven tarmac. One had a drain in the middle.

Our tennis was abominable at first but we laughed and had fun every Saturday.

And my elegant young man, of the slightly bent legs, was a member. It was hate at first sight, well, on his part. I still desired him, but he was such a good tennis player he could have been a champion if he'd had the opportunity, and it must have been annoying for him to wait for a court while four giggling girls were rabbiting about. Several girls had their eye on him, he was so aloof and unattainable. One very pretty girl I knew he liked made the mistake of confiding in her mother her desire for this young man. She was in comfortable circumstances and Mama bought two theatre tickets suggesting her daughter invite the young man, saying the tickets were complimentary ones. I think he was on the point of asking this girl for a date himself, but as soon as she made her suggestion of the trip to the theatre, he was away like a startled fawn. Well, it didn't show like that, but as a student of human nature I knew it when he politely refused the trip to the theatre.

I had to play my cards more carefully. The way to a man's heart is through his stomach. Well, I couldn't cook and couldn't ask mother to make dainty cakes for the tennis club refreshments; in her book one didn't ask a man for anything, or let him know one's desires. Cooking was out and he looked as though he never ate in any case. What other domestic delight could I think of? Then one day I heard him admire a tennis pullover another player was wearing. My knitting was almost as poor as my cooking, but some girls knitted for the sheer pleasure of it. If I knitted a pullover for him I could casually say I just happened to have some knitting on hand. The elegant young man was called Charles. He had a large good-looking quiet friend, Alfred, who had his eyes shyly on Marjorie, and Marjorie, to help me, said she would knit a pullover for Alfred, a pair would look more of a club member's gesture than a single gift would. The latter might appear to have an ulterior motive. Someone showed me how to do cable stitch and join three colours of wool round the neck for I only knew the tying-a-knot-in-the-wool way.

Marjorie's garment was all white and quickly done. Mine took a long time, and as I could never make up my mind about quantities or measurements, always afraid I should spoil the ship for a ha'porth of tar, I kept adding to the length.

Finally it was completed and the whole family, for once, admired my handiwork. Marjorie just popped her pullover in a bag, but mine was a work of love for a special person, an ensnarement present. I bought a presentation box, layers of tissue, drove my family mad packing and unpacking it to make it look professional, and jumped down Mother's throat when she gently suggested she would squeeze it very carefully through warm soap flakes for me. I stood over her like nemesis while she pressed it under a damp cloth. The great Saturday arrived for the presentation. Marjorie squashed her bag in her tennis holdall, one of the boys tied mine up as though it had come from Harrods and we set off, much to Mother's relief and amusement – relief to get me out of the house with the thing, amusement because Father had said the pullover was so weighty the young man would have to be mighty strong to keep it in a vertical position.

The whole club knew we were knitting these pullovers and after the handing-out ceremony, with the right amount of shy casualness from me, we all sat in deck chairs and waited for Charlie and Alfred to reappear, as Adonises. Chas had wanted to pay me for the wool, but I airily said it was some I had by me. (Years later in a moment of temper he told me he felt I wanted the money for the wool really.)

One young man came rushing out after a few minutes and he was laughing, I couldn't think why. Then he said, 'They're coming,' and then I knew why, for the whole of the club became hysterical. Alf's pullover hardly fitted across his broad chest and was as short as a miniature bolero. Chas's creation, my labour of love, sweat and toil, came down past his knees and it was full enough for a maternity frock. The two young men took the poses of male models, accentuating the comedy of the situation. Marjorie was choking with laughter too, and in me rose a feeling so murderous towards this creature I had suffered for, that I wished for an axe to cleave him in two. I said casually, although I was choking with misery, that I could see it needed a little alteration and I stuffed it in my holdall. Silence greeted me on my arrival home. Mother had known it was too big but she couldn't advise me. I wanted to be on the safe side, and of course, I never listened to reason. Well I listened to advice but I never took it.

At every opportunity after that I had a dig at Charles and since I was quicker-tongued than he, I got great satisfaction from this. He was sensible enough not to ask how the pull-over was getting on.

Came the day of the tennis-club outing, we were all going to the sea by coach. I had seen in a magazine a beautiful picture of a hand-knitted bathing-costume. The wool, a new invention, would remain unaffected by sea water. It was very expensive but I decided I would cut a dash, this time working strictly to measurement. I gave up my precious books and night after night worked on this creation. With my gingery hair went a milk white skin of body. No one of course had ever seen this except Mother and my sisters, but I was the only one in the family with this whiteness and it was remarked on. In my jade green and white bathing-suit, Chas would feel overcome, and I could be suitably off hand with him.

The suit fitted beautifully and the weather was so hot I thought I would just wear a frock over it. I wouldn't be going in the sea, I couldn't swim, just a few awkward strokes. No, I would drape myself on the beach for his admiration. Mother was horrified that this was to be the whole of my outfit and so I left by the front door letting her assume I had gone upstairs to make myself more respectable.

When we arrived at the seaside everybody made for the sea, so there was no one left to admire me and I was per-suaded to come into the water just to frolic. The weather was so hot I would dry off in the sun afterwards. I went into the sea which was lovely and warm, Marjorie was Australian-crawling in the distance, always a strong and expert swim-mer. Alfred was splashing about and I thought I would swim to him and splash him. His look became very nasty and he shouted, 'Get away, get away,' but still I went on chasing him, when suddenly two hands grabbed me round the knees and dragged me under the water. I was choking and struggling and fighting to get to the surface when I heard Marjorie's frantic voice. 'Keep under the water until I can help you, your costume's stretched and you look naked.' So much for the expensive wool. Marjorie helped a crestfallen and miserable sister back to the beach, the costume which Marjorie was holding in a bunch round my neck was also down almost to my ankles. Again hysteria from the club, including Chas. Again I wished for an axe to cleave him in two.

It was difficult to know what was to be done, embarrassment all round, for I couldn't go home naked under a frock. Suppose the wind blew. Then a young man appeared from some bushes and handed me his pants. 'It's the best I can do,' he said. He was a young man to whom I was always very condescending, yet he was the one to help me in my trouble. I came home in the warm male garment to be met by a Mother who was disgusted. She assumed I had played 'fast and loose' and she almost choked to find I had worn a pair of man's pants. The fact that he had taken them off for me to wear suggested to her something so depraved that for the first time in my life she looked as though she wanted to slap me. I was in tears. What a rotten day, what a rotten homecoming. Why did everything turn into a calamity for me? Then I thought of the thing which would make mother happy and relieved again. She would know she had a respectable daughter again, that I was aware of the proprieties. 'I put John's pants on back to front, Mum, you'll be pleased to know.' It was as though I had dropped a bombshell and confirmed all her dark suspicions. She choked and said she never thought she'd live to see the day, etc., etc. What had I done wrong now? Of course I had mentioned the 'opening', always a necessary, and apparently evil, part of a man's apparel.

20 Holy honeymoon

Charles and I were still distant but polite enemies, then on New Year's Eve he suggested it would be a good idea to see the New Year in up in the City. Although I was on my own when he asked me I knew he meant all the gang and so I passed the word around. I thought he looked a bit surprised when he met about twelve of us at the top of the Grove but we started off in fine spirits. None of us had any money but we liked walking. I was in a mood to see humour in everything and our laughter carried us along through the East End into the West End. We were walking back through Fleet Street when the unhappy silence of Chas made me remark, 'Cheer up, if you see the New Year in with such a straight face you'll be miserable all the year.' Whereupon to my frightened surprise and the startled amazement of the gang, he grabbed hold of me and dragged me across Fleet Street.

He ran with me up a little side turning where we knocked the lid off a dustbin, startling but pleasing some thin-looking cats, until finally tired with running I followed him like a squaw to the 23 bus stop, and he was silent until we reached my house. By the twitching of the lace curtains I knew that Mother (ostrich-like she always thought herself invisible and I never told her otherwise) was already ensconced in the public gallery. My caveman began utterance. 'Everything is an almighty joke to you isn't it? You knew I wanted to be alone with you and you humiliated me by inviting all the crowd. Well that's it, I will not put myself in this position again.' Humbly (that would annoy Mother but she could only see not hear in her theatre box), I said, 'This is so sudden,' which was the wrong reply. But finally I reassured Charles that I really had no idea how he felt and that I would be very happy to meet him alone on our next date.

Thus it came to pass, my fate was decided, and I was certain that from then on our love would run a smooth course.

Chas had worked all his working life at an exporters in Farringdon Street, but had progressed, if he had progressed at all, very slowly. He had been conscientious, attending night school regularly and was the proud possessor of all the shipping certificates necessary for him to become an import and export clerk. His firm, however, were connected through the management with a church at Purley in Surrey, the organist at this church also holding a position of trust with the firm and it seemed to be staffed by members of the congregation. Since we were serious there seemed no prospects for my future bridegroom at his firm and he looked elsewhere for a job in shipping. Luck was against us for there was a slump on at the time and a friend of his suggested he learn to be a waiter. The work was hard and long, the wages twelve shillings per week but the tips could be very worthwhile, and so, for love, he took this terrible job which I thought was tantamount to slavery.

He had very little time off for courting and I would go to his restaurant and spend a few hours there two evenings a week. I resented having to pay for my courting, although I enjoyed the food, and I was getting fatter through eating it. Chas was getting thinner, if that were possible. He was long hours on his feet, and the staff food was vile, quite different from what was served in the restaurant, but he was a good waiter, deft and handsome in his uniform. Things that happened to him there amused me greatly, but were tragedies to him, and it was difficult not to laugh at the expression on his face when mishaps occurred.

One night a man ordered a baked apple with syrup sauce and when Chas arrived at the table, the plate was on his tray, but there was no baked apple. Just like Charlie Chaplin he searched everywhere, but had to go back for a replacement. He would have had to anyway because he could hardly dust off a syrupy baked apple. The man finished his meal, I watched Chas help him on with his overcoat and as the man put his hand in his overcoat pocket, I knew where the baked apple was. The man was led off expostulating to be de-syruped, Chas was nearly in tears, and I pretended I had dropped my gloves under the table. Poor Chas, he also had to pay for the baked apple. It had slid into the open pocket as Chas made his great swing round from the service door.

Another evening a girl was sitting at a table with a young man. They were engrossed in each other, obviously in love, and I watched them enviously. She was wearing a beautifully embroidered muslin blouse, transparent-looking where there was no embroidery. It was gorgeous. Chas came in with their salad and as he bent down over the table the bottle of oil tipped up, and down this girl's blouse went the oil. She burst into tears, she could have done nothing worse for a man like mine, he was nearly in tears too; he started to wipe her bosom with his white cloth and then leapt back startled at his near immorality. She too was led off in tears.

One night a very red and tottery man sat at my table and ordered whitebait. I thought he was having whiting and when this multitude of tiny grey fish with large closed eyes was served up he must have seen my surprised expression for he began to toss them in the air with his fork laughing and saying, 'I love them little fishes, them little fishes, my dear, I love.' He was led away by Chas and the supervisor. They apologised to me and said they wouldn't have served him if they had known he was inebriated, but I think it was my expression which started the man off on his childish pranks.

Well, someone had to lay the foundation of the family fortunes so I obtained a better paid job nearer home. It was with a large food firm and considered to be a plum job. Such jobs were never advertised, going to families who 'spoke' for each other, but I happened to write in at a time when no relation of the office staff was available. The factory foreman took on the staff. Since no office staff had been taken on for years and years, and there was no interviewer specially for them, whereas factory staff were large in number, I was interviewed by this foreman. He was very sensitive about his baldness and lived permanently in a large grey cap. He wore a white overall and we sat in a grimy little waiting-room for the interview. Progressively, it had been decided that future staff should undergo an intelligence test, an innovation, and this foreman was to test me. The trouble was he didn't understand the test himself, and the cards which should have gone in order were so jumbled up by him that the questions made no sense, in any case I doubt if he was bright enough to recognise the answers. In the end, for he didn't seem to know whether I was employing him or he me – he was asking me the answers to the questions – I suggested I sort the cards out for him. He was so relieved when I told him which questions to ask me and in which order, that he happily told me I was employed if I passed my medical. I passed the medical, but when I finally started work I felt the medical was to see whether I could survive such conditions.

It was like working in a hot damp cellar. The electric light was on all day, and outside the area window hung a dirty-looking glass reflector. I was being paid an enormous wage but didn't work at all until about three o'clock when the invoices came in and these took me a couple of hours. The senior shorthand typist did a couple of letters each day, or so it seemed to me. In the main office men appeared to be working but the girl in that office spent her time in close, whispered conversation with one of the married clerks. The engineer brought me orchids from his greenhouse, and the little orchid in the tumbler on my desk kept me going. We had lovely lunches in the director's dining-room, and only the fact that I was to be married kept me there. I was bored. They didn't need me to do a few simple invoices. I was getting money under false pretences and so, in my opinion, were the rest of the office staff, though there were a few male exceptions. I thought the owners and directors were on the millionaire side and I felt the waste of money and time acutely and wondered if what they sold could not have been made cheaper for the populace.

Until the Friday of my wedding, I had not purchased my

bridal outfit. I decided I would not be married in white, with bridesmaids, the money would be better spent on our home. Chas and I had nearly broken up at the time of flat-hunting. He was tired, for he said the thick carpets at the restaurant wore his feet away, and I felt very shy about living in a house with a landlady. Finally we obtained a flat for 22s. 6d. per week at St Johns, near Lewisham, and purchased a walnut bedroom suite, with a his and hers wardrobe – my wardrobe was immense with huge bevelled glass doors – an oak dining-room suite, two leather arm-chairs, lino, one large rug for the sitting-room, a coffee table, a kitchen table and chairs, and two rugs for the bedroom. Our beautiful home cost £56.

Amy came with me to Ilford to choose my wedding suit. I could find nothing I liked and finally settled for a very expensive frock in heavy turquoise marocain. I wasn't really enamoured with it but it was so well cut it made my figure look very attractive. Passing the hat shop I saw in the window a beautiful Java straw picture hat with a turquoise ribbon band and binding, and this, with the dress, made a wedding outfit.

On the Saturday morning my father appeared all innocent and got ready for cricket saying he didn't know I wanted him to give me away. This upset me and he said he would give me away, but it would be the last time. Mother said he didn't want to give any of his daughters away as it upset him too much. I knew it was because he preferred his cricket matches, but I didn't want any further arguments.

As we set off for the church, everyone else having gone, my father began calculating at what time he would arrive at his cricket match if the clergyman hurried it up, and in this mood we arrived at the church to find the vicar had also gone into Kent to a cricket match. My father brightened visibly at the verger's information and was about to make off with a clear conscience when the new curate appeared. I felt like making off somewhere myself and would have done if it hadn't taken so long to arrange my hat. I wanted to get a bit of wear from it in public. The curate restrained my father, apologising for the vicar's absence, and said I had been omitted from the book in error; he had never yet conducted a marriage service but he would do his best for the young people.

We walked down the aisle following the curate, now garbed in his wedding regalia. I felt something strange flapping against my leg and looking over my shoulder saw two inches of my new blue petticoat hanging down. I had a large safety-pin in my knickers, so they were safe; perhaps people would look at my hat. We reached my bridegroom and his brother. They had come out of the front pew and were standing with their backs to us as we approached. I thought Charles seemed to be swaying a bit and then I saw his face. He was as white as a sheet and his brother was supporting him with his hand on his arm. I thought, my goodness, what with one thing and another and now this, I'm the one who is supposed to be white and trembling, not him, and through my smile I felt I was clenching my teeth. I remember nothing of the service and then we were kneeling at the altar being given advice on our future life by this saint-like boy. It was the wrong advice as it turned out, we should have been given a hint on other hazards – though perhaps not in a holy place.

As we came out of church I saw my father haring it up the road to the bus stop, and thought he shouldn't be galloping like that on such a hot day. It really was sweltering. My husband had revived now that the worst was over, or he thought the worst was over, and catching sight of an old friend in the crowd he gave an enthusiastic wave, knocking my Ascot hat sideways. In a wave of pent-up emotion I gave him a mighty thump on his arm. He should have been leaning over me in a state of great love and joy and not waving to one of his old football mates, and to my utter horror and the amusement of the spectators, he gave me a fiendish look of hate and thumped me in return. That is why we have no photographs of my wedding. The thumping one I destroyed and wished many times I had saved it for future evidence. 'And you see this, Judge . . .'

We had organised sherry, spirits, light wine and refreshments at no. 13 but against all advice I refused to have beer. Beer to me was common and on this sweltering hot day all the men guests, and some of the ladies, wanted only a cool beer. It would have been ice cold in the cellar. Fortunately for them we left early and then I heard there was a rush round to Chas's house for the crates his people had ordered unknown to me. What a cat I was really.

Chas's brother Robin saw us off at the main line station and I felt quite flat and miserable and wished I could have been going home with him. I suspect poor Chas felt the same. We had a late lunch on the train but I couldn't eat mine because the perspiration was dripping down the waiter's nose on to the food.

We had booked at a hotel on the honeymoon Isle of Wight. I did not know it catered for religious conventions; a girl at the office had given me the address informing me it was a heavenly place in which to embark on the sanctity of married life. I discovered later she was a religious fanatic.

We took a taxi from the station. I thought the driver looked surprised, and the next day we were too, for in the dusk we had not realised our hotel was bang slap up against the taxi rank. The driver did run us round one or two streets first though.

We were greeted by the proprietress with the information that she was full to the ceiling with a religious convention and had been forced to put us in the annexe. It had only thin asbestos walls and she warned us, or thought we would like to know, that everything, just everything could be heard through these walls. So with that cheerful beginning we washed and came down to dinner, the object of many staring eyes.

The dining-room was full of dark-suited whispering clergymen. At the next table to us was a large red-faced bishop. The waitress called through a hatch, 'One gent's, one lady's dinner, please.' The lady's dinner was minuscule, the gent's small. I was absolutely starving and finished it as though it were an appetiser. My husband couldn't touch his, the ferry had made him sick. I saw his dinner being removed sadly, for I was too shy to start on his after devouring my own. I whispered that if my meal was to be smaller, my bill should be smaller too. This worried my husband and he made a large shushing noise and the clergymen looked over and ogled us. Unfortunately because Chas left his dinner, for the rest of the stay his meals were minuscule too; they obviously kidded themselves they had been giving him too large a meal for a man.

We went for a walk on the front and sat on a seat not knowing what to say to one another. I got up and put some pennies in a fun machine. This brought my husband to life for he thought it was a sheer waste of money, and I wondered if he thought I was going to squander the housekeeping when I received it.

Finally we went back to the hotel to commence our nuptials. We had been very modern, or so we thought. We would get some capital behind us before commencing a family. He, being the man, it was left to him to arrange the non-arrival of a family. He was as green as I was and had visited a seedy shop in Villiers Street. All this I learned many moons later. The man behind the counter had a 'Do you want to buy a dirty picture' look about him, and when my husband enquired about sheaths, the man asked, 'How many?' This shocked my husband and he said he only required one, a good one. Then the man surprised Chas further by asking, 'What size?' Now, my darling had no idea that such things came in sizes, and he had to admit that he didn't know the size. The man then scrutinised him closely and said, 'You'll want small' and sold him what I thought was only to be compared with a Michelin X tyre.

Chas went to the bathroom while I put on my beautiful wedding nightie and I was sitting up in bed when he returned with a look of pain on his weary face. Struggling with this tyre it had shot behind the bath and he had spent ages on his hands and knees looking for it. When finally it was on successfully he cried out in agony because he felt he was being strangled. I thought this was a strange word to choose, but he got into bed and I put my arms round him. He looked

185

worn out and closed his eyes. Before he fell asleep he looked round the poky room and said sadly, 'It is a pity, I was looking forward to these two weeks just to be able to get some good nights' sleep.' I lay awake and wondered how many bridegrooms had looked forward to their honeymoon for the sake of a good night's rest. Then I became all maternal and thought about the long hours he worked. He really hadn't the physique for it, and he had taken the wretched job so that we could save up and get married. I made up my mind to give him a happy fortnight. After all, we had years and years in front of us. Then the moths began to arrive, great furry flapping creatures, and it seemed almost dawn before an unsatisfied, but saintly, bride gained repose.

Suddenly we were awakened by shouts and screaming and strange language. The bishop in the next room suffered from nightmares. According to the proprietress he had suffered mightily in the jungle as a missionary. The next day we were passing through the gardens when the bishop's umbrella caught fire. He had gone to sleep using it as a parasol, still smoking his pipe. I would have let it burn as retaliation for my sleepless night but my husband, always a boy scout, put the flames out. Much giggling took place for the rest of the time among all those holy black-coated workers.

We were getting a little more bored each day until we met the two young men. Charming creatures they were, very fond of one another, and we arranged to play tennis with them. My husband brightened up for he was bored with nothing to do, and we played some jolly matches with them. My husband would not let any ball escape him and straining to reach a high ball behind him he overbalanced, slid on his racquet, sprained his ankle and gashed his hand on the gravelled court. He possessed one of those faces which register pain so acutely it is frightening to see. The two young men made their adieus, they had to catch a coach, I must take my husband to the doctor immediately, they advised. I tied his brown shoes together and slung them round my neck. I took his jacket, racquet, balls under my arm, and placing his arm round my shoulder we began our tortured journey back to the hotel. His groans and our slow progress made us a spectacle for the onlookers and, becoming acutely embarrassed at his face, and annoyed at the circumstances in which I found myself, I said 'What on earth did you want to try to reach such an impossible ball for?' Sensing my feeling he became rather insulting, or so I thought, about my tennis capabilities, and I said 'Well, surely there's no need to make the fuss you are making?' He stopped dead in the street and began to shout about my callousness and lack of feeling and as we had an audience I apologised. I didn't mean my apology but it was the only way to get him to resume our uneven pace, for he was tall, I was short and loaded. We were all in white and I felt we looked like two ghostly survivors from a safari. I only needed a jar of tiddlers to match his slung shoes round my neck.

When I helped him into the dining-room that evening, he winced and groaned until he found a comfortable place for his sprained foot. His hand was bandaged and the ogling clergymen must have thought it was Passion Sunday. They were probably pleased they were married to the Virgin Mary. 'Such a pity to meet with an accident on one's honeymoon,' one said to me. I would liked to have said, 'Yes, a trifle restricting,' but I knew my place.

I went to see my dear mother on my return. She said I didn't appear to have enjoyed my honeymoon. I said, 'Well, not really,' and she said, confidentially, 'I could have told you it was overrated.' Her first and last mention of such a subject to me.

On that visit I accompanied her to the Mothers' Union. True I wasn't a mother, but I was her married daughter. The woman in charge was a large county type out of the top drawer, very interested and helpful to the mothers of the poor. She had one of those high-faluting voices which the music hall comics like to imitate. Each member was given a copy of the Union, and each time this good lady brought out the required number of copies she was a few short. She fetched more copies and before she commenced her lecture she said, 'Well, have you all had it?' and I whispered to

Mother as I looked at the poor toothless grannies and tired worn out mums, 'Not recently,' and the little granny next to me heard and it was difficult to stop her cackling. Mother looked very disapproving but there was a twinkle in her eye. I was a married woman now. To mention it as 'it' was not too wicked provided I still whispered.

The granny's giggling seemed to excite and bring to life the mothers sitting near us and they edged closer so as to be included in the fun. My mother, because she *was* my mother, knew that all I needed, with my sense of the ridiculous, was a foil or stooge to turn the meeting into Bedlam, and because she was fearful our laughter would get out of hand during the lady visitor's talk, she poured calm upon the chaos by asking if anyone knew what the talk would be about that afternoon. 'The beauty of Woochechersheer,' said one mother.

The very way she pronounced Worcestershire brought instantly and vividly to my mind the frightened little blond boy of my childhood gazing at the broken bottle with the brown river of sauce oozing from it, and the same boy running in terror after the coal cart carrying the injured child. In a blinding flash of memory I knew – it was uncanny how I was so sure – that I had married that boy. It seemed those pictures had been in my mind all my life yet I had never realised before it was Chas. Although it was difficult to equate him with the heroes in Elinor Glyn's popular novels, I was sure our meeting and marriage had been pre-destined and I was anxious to rush home and tell him the exciting news. Perhaps we would have a rich life together. I would go to work the very next day and save up all my money so that he could leave the slavery of his job.

I could hardly contain myself whilst waiting to tell him all my lovely plans for the future and I sat at the sitting-room window in the dark waiting his return. The clock on the mantel-shelf ticked loudly. Midnight passed and still no Charles. Finally, at two a.m., when I was dizzy gazing at the stars, I saw him turn into the road. He had worked later than usual, had missed the train and had walked some of the way. I sat in silence while he ate his supper for my mother always said, 'Let a man eat his meal first before you talk to him after a hard day.' While he was in the bathroom I went to bed and put on my honeymoon nightie. I could hear his noisy ablutions; he was like a drowning man when he rinsed his face, for he took in great gasping breaths as he splashed water over it – so much water that it ran down his elbows in rivers, and he seemed to scrub up like a surgeon.

He never glanced at me as he got into bed and switched off the light. 'Say Worcestershire,' I said to him, taking his hand. He flung my hand aside and shouted, 'Now look here, I've had a real sod of a day, I've just got to get some sleep, save your stupid games for some other time.' I should have taken his advice but I was so anxious to know if my intuition was right that I babbled on about the boy in Chrisp Street and the boy on the coal-cart. He didn't seem a bit thrilled to know he *was* the boy I had always remembered but just remarked that it was typical of me to remind him of the saddest day of his life when his brother was injured in the raid and his school-friends were killed. Thinking to cheer him up, I said didn't he think it was strange we had met at all, that I was able to join his tennis club when I couldn't play tennis. He switched on the bedside light (such a luxury we had thought). In its pink glow with my lovely nightie on I knew with my smile of love I must look a picture of blushing willingness. He raised himself on one elbow and leaned over me, ready, I thought, to take me in his arms and say passionately, 'Darling you are right, it was *meant* to be.' Suddenly and belligerently he said, as though he was speaking to an idiot, 'As secretary of that club I knew we were short of funds, I let you join only because we needed the money.' And he turned his back on me and put out the light.

Shoes Were for Sunday 40p
Molly Weir

'Poverty is a very exacting teacher, and I had been taught well.

The asphalt jungle of the Glasgow tenements was the setting for Molly Weir's childhood.

Despite crippling poverty and overcrowding, there was endless fun – from impromptu recitations to the delights of the annual fair.

And dominating her life was Grannie, whose tough, independen spirit gave Molly so rich a life in such pitiful surroundings.

'Will delight not only admirers of Molly Weir as a TV personality, but all who enjoy recollections of childhood . . . as, combining deep feeling with surface gaiety, she tells of her early years' BIRMINGHAM POST

'This is a rare book' OBSERVER

James Herriot

If Only They Could Talk 50p

The genial misadventures of James Herriot, a young vet in the lovely Yorkshire Dales, are enough to make a cat laugh – let alone the animals, if only they could talk.

'This warm, joyous and often hilarious chronicle shines with love of life . . . Triumphs, failures and merely embarrassing incidents are all told with equal candour. There is humour everywhere' NEW YORK TIMES

'One of the best countryside books I have read in years . . . full of life and fun with an imaginative touch which makes the most of the fine scenery and rich characters of the Dales' OXFORD MAIL

It Shouldn't Happen to a Vet 50p

'Imagine a *Dr Finlay's Casebook* scripted by Richard Gordon and Thurlow Craig and starring Ronnie Corbett and you will understand why James Herriot is on to a winner . . . a delightful new collection of stories' SUNDAY EXPRESS

'His easy and at times excruciatingly funny case-history narratives must rate as country classics and he throws in a stumbling, awkward courtship for good measure' FARMERS' WEEKLY

Let Sleeping Vets Lie 50p

The hilarious revelations of James Herriot, the now famous vet in the Yorkshire Dales, continue his happy story of everyday trials and tribulations with unwilling animal patients and their richly diverse owners.

'He can tell a good story against himself, and his pleasure in the beauty of the countryside in which he works is infectious' DAILY TELEGRAPH

'Full of funny anecdotes and great old farming characters. A real breath of the countryside' DAILY EXPRESS

Selected bestsellers

☐ **Let Sleeping Vets Lie** James Herriot 50p
☐ **Jaws** Peter Benchley 50p
☐ **Slay-Ride** Dick Francis 45p
☐ **The Tower** Richard Martin Stern 50p
  (filmed as *The Towering Inferno*)
☐ **Open Season** David Osborn 50p
☐ **The Man with the Golden Gun** Ian Fleming 40p
☐ **Gold** (previously *Gold Mine*) Wilbur Smith 40p
☐ **Airport** Arthur Hailey 50p
☐ **Mandingo** Kyle Onstott 50p
☐ **Royal Flash** George MacDonald Fraser 40p
☐ **The Poseidon Adventure** Paul Gallico 60p
☐ **Penmarric** Susan Howatch 75p
☐ **Lady of Quality** Georgette Heyer 50p
☐ **The Frightened Bride** Barbara Cartland 40p
☐ **Fuzz** Ed McBain 30p
☐ **Jonathan Livingston Seagull** Richard Bach 50p
☐ **The Spy Who Came In from the Cold** John le Carré 40p
☐ **Princess of Celle** Jean Plaidy 60p
☐ **Bury My Heart at Wounded Knee** Dee Brown 95p
☐ **The Little Prince** Antoine de Saint-Exupéry 35p
☐ **The Maltese Falcon** Dashiell Hammett 45p

All these books are available at your bookshop or newsagent;
or can be obtained direct from the publisher
Just tick the titles you want and fill in the form below

Pan Books Cavaye Place, London SW10 9PG
Send purchase price plus 15p for the first book and 5p for each
additional book, to allow for postage and packing

Name (block letters) ―――――――――――――――――――――――――

Address ―――――――――――――――――――――――――――――――

―――――――――――――――――――――――――――――――――――

While every effort is made to keep prices low, it is sometimes
necessary to increase prices at short notice. Pan Books reserve the
right to show on covers new retail prices which may differ from
those advertised in the text or elsewhere